S

ASTR

Should Have Told You

A DAVID AND CHARLES BOOK
© Quarto Publishing plc 2024

David and Charles is an imprint of David and Charles, Ltd
Suite A, Tourism House, Pynes Hill, Exeter, EX2 5WS

Conceived, edited, and designed by Quarto Publishing, an imprint of
The Quarto Group, 1 Triptych Place, London, SE1 9SH

First published in the UK and USA in 2024

A catalogue record for this book is available from the British Library.

ISBN-13: 9781446313428 paperback
ISBN-13: 9781446313435 EPUB

This book has been printed on paper from approved suppliers and
made from pulp from sustainable sources.

Printed in China

10 9 8 7 6 5 4 3 2 1

Editor: Charlene Fernandes
Designer: Eliana Holder
Copyeditor: Caroline West
Designer (layout): Karin Skånberg
Illustrations: Bruna Sailor Broo
Art director: Martina Calvio
Publisher: Lorraine Dickey

David and Charles publishes high-quality books on a wide range of
subjects. For more information visit www.davidandcharles.com.

Share your makes with us on social media using #dandcbooks and
follow us on Facebook and Instagram by searching for @dandcbooks.

Layout of the digital edition of this book may vary depending on
reader hardware and display settings.

Stuff Your
ASTROLOGER
Should Have Told You

The brutally honest truth behind
the bad traits of each star sign

DAVID & CHARLES

www.davidandcharles.com

Contents

Meet Alise   6

Introduction   8

Aries *March 21–April 19*   14

Taurus *April 20–May 20*   26

Gemini *May 21–June 20*   38

Cancer *June 21–July 22*   50

Leo *July 23–August 22*   62

Virgo *August 23–September 22*   74

Libra *September 23–October 22*   86

Scorpio *October 23–November 21*   98

Sagittarius *November 22–December 21*   110

Capricorn *December 22–January 19*   122

Aquarius *January 20–February 18*   134

Pisces *February 19–March 20*   146

Index   158

Credits and acknowledgments   160

Meet Alise

When I don't have my head in the stars, I'm a comedian based out of Brooklyn, New York, best known for my years of work writing the Betches Sup Newsletter and my Headgum podcast "Go Touch Grass," where I break down the week's internet news alongside my cohost and dear friend Milly Tamarez. I started my comedy journey ten years ago now, moving to New York after falling in love with improv in college. From there, I moved through the ranks at the Upright Citizens Brigade Theater, eventually joining one of their house improv teams where I performed for several very happy years.

During that time, I also worked on my stand-up and solo career, developing my original live comedy show "The Roast of Your Teenage Self," which toured the country to sold-out crowds and has been featured annually as part of the New York Comedy Festival. It is there that I developed a penchant for light-hearted roasting that eventually led to this book. I truly believe that setting aside time to laugh at ourselves and make light of our shortcomings is one of the best and most healing things a person can do.

In fact, writing the Taurus chapter of this book helped me get out of a rut and move on from a job that was no longer serving me. By roasting myself, I actually helped myself.

In addition to my stage career, I've also been a working actress in film and television for several years, having appeared on shows like Hulu's *Difficult People, The Marvelous Mrs. Maisel*, and Stephen Colbert's *Tooning Out The News*. If you can't already tell by the length of this bio, I'm a writer whose work has appeared on Betches, Reductress, PureWow, and Jezebel and in the comedy anthology Notes From The Bathroom Line. My adult puzzle book *Hello, I'm a F****** Puzzle Genius* was released in 2020 and my first astrology book *Zodiac Connections* was released with Thunder Bay Press in 2023. I got my start in astrology while writing for Betches, covering their weekly horoscopes and eventually moving on to write their weekly astrology newsletter, "Blame it On Retrograde."

The road from comedy writer and actress to astrologer hasn't been the most direct, but I've certainly enjoyed the ride. Like many others in my age group (millennial and proud), I started getting interested in astrology several years ago as a diversion from some of the more stressful aspects of my life. Rather than seeing my natal chart, star sign, or horoscope as a prescription to be followed, I've always viewed astrology as an interesting framework through which to view the world. By looking to my star sign (Taurus, by the way) or reviewing my birth chart, I've found that what I'm really thinking about is myself, looking to the future that I'd like to build, and the values that drive what I do.

Also, it's fun! And—despite what I say in this book about my star sign being boring—I do love fun. I hope you have as much fun being roasted by this book as I did writing it. Now if you'll excuse me, I have to get back to work. Like I said, I'm a Taurus.

Alise

Introduction

Greetings stargazer

If you're reading this book, chances are you've decided you need to be taken down a peg or two. Or you're so baffled by the thought that anyone could have anything bad to say about you that you had to pick up this book and watch someone try (*cough*Leo*cough*). Either way, you're welcome.

In these pages you will not find your typical astrological breakdown of the signs, which tends to focus on all the great things each star sign has to offer. Nope. We've seen enough of that. In *this* book you'll learn about the dark side of each sign—from the rageaholics, to the self-important snobs, to megalomaniacal sociopaths masking themselves as "free spirits"—and finally get real about what each sign is *not* bringing to the table. Sure, it may sting to see your sign's flaws laid out so honestly, but at least you're in bad company.

Within these pages you'll find a chapter dedicated to each sign. We start with an overview of each sign's foibles and worst qualities, then dig deeper, outlining exactly what pitfalls they face at work, at home, while traveling, and, of course, in love. Is your sign a commitment-phobe destined to flit between short-term relationships and leave a string of broken hearts in their wake? Or is your sign a serial monogamist clinger who will waste hours—even years—of their life on the wrong person just because they can't bear the upheaval of a breakup? Turn to your star sign's chapter to find out.

Each chapter also comes with a list of five notorious individuals that encapsulate that sign's most nefarious qualities. We all need something to aspire to, right? We also include information about moon signs and rising signs because, despite what Big Astrology may try to tell you, the signs can wreak havoc on your life no matter where they appear in your chart. We end each chapter with information on cusps—those tricky little rascals born at the intersection of two signs that thereby take on some of the negative qualities of each.

Before you begin, it'd probably be best to define some key concepts for the amateur astrologers in the room. Taurus, you may want to take notes. We all know you can be a bit slow on the uptake.

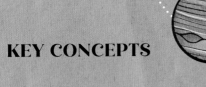

KEY CONCEPTS

Ruling planet

Each sign in the Zodiac has its own planetary master. A sign's ruling planet is key to that sign's personality, and its movements through the cosmos have a big impact on how it interacts with the world. Here's a quick primer on each of the ruling planets and the signs that do their bidding.

Mercury

Mercury rules over Gemini and Virgo and represents communication, changeability, thought, and reason. Mercury is all about thought and intellect, meaning its Zodiac minions are far more infatuated with ideas than people and always speak their mind. (Translation: They hurt feelings and don't even realize it.)

Venus

Venus is the planet of love and beauty and rules over Taurus and Libra. While "love and beauty" may sound nice, Venus's influence often means its charges are overly obsessed with both. These signs spend their whole life in the pursuit of romance, comfort, and aesthetic beauty, but it may all end up a facade. In short, they make great influencers.

Mars

Mars rules over Aries and symbolizes drive, desire, intensity, and aggression. This planet is named after the Roman god of war, so it should come as no surprise that it is combative, survivalist, and slightly animalistic in its influence. In short, the red planet's influence will make anyone a hothead.

Jupiter

Jupiter rules over Sagittarius and is all about expansion and excess (it is the largest planet in the Solar System after all). This gargantuan glutton is obsessed with having a good time and the concept of more, more, more. All that to say, when Jupiter is in the driver's seat, you might want to watch your wallet.

Saturn

Stuffy Saturn rules over Capricorn and all of the Zodiac with an iron fist. It is astrology's disapproving father and is all about strictness, rules, and regulations. It symbolizes structure and hates deviations from the norm. No fun here! Get back to work!

Uranus

Quirky Uranus floats through the Solar System at a tilt and likes to turn everything on its head. In modern astrology it rules over rebellious Aquarius (to the extent that Aquarius will let itself be ruled) and symbolizes freedom, change, and rebellion. When Uranus appears in the sky, know that things are going to get weird.

Neptune

Neptune rules over Pisces in modern astrology and is the planet of idealism, dreams, and artistry. It puts a hazy veil over everything, making it hard to discern truth from lies, dreams from reality. Think you're getting work done when Neptune takes the wheel? Think again.

Pluto

Yes, modern astrology still considers Pluto a planet (sorry scientists), and that planet is the symbol of transformation, destruction, death, and rebirth. This planet rules over Scorpio, accounting for this sign's intense, slightly dark-sided nature. It's not their fault! Their planet makes them that way.

The Sun

The Sun in astrology represents the ego, vitality, and self, so it's no wonder it rules over self-obsessed Leo. It sees itself as the center of the universe because...well...it is! Hard to argue with that.

The Moon

The Moon symbolizes your internal self and emotional power and rules over the sign Cancer. It is all about inner feelings and depth, making Cancers particularly susceptible to changing emotions, doom, and gloom. If you're someone who always cries at movies, you probably have the Moon to thank.

Elements

Each of the 12 Zodiac signs can be sorted into one of four elements—earth, water, fire, and air. Your element affects a sign's personality and how it experiences the world. Signs of the same element often see the world through a similar lens, while signs of opposing elements can have difficulty relating to one another.

Earth

Earth signs tend to be grounded folks who experience the world through physical sensations. If it's not right in front of them, they don't believe it, meaning they can be a bit stubborn and unyielding in their worldviews.

Water

Water signs are emotional people who experience the world through their inner feelings. Like an ocean, they want to go deep with everyone and are highly sensitive. Even the smallest disturbance to their emotional state can have ripple effects for days.

Fire

Fire signs are action-oriented people who experience the world through instinct. They are constantly on the go and hate the feeling of standing still. These signs are fun and exciting, but they can often leave others feeling burned out.

Air

Air signs are intellectuals who experience the world through ideas and thoughts. They love a good conversation, but fly away the moment feelings or emotions come into play. They can be high-minded and above-it-all, making them hard to pin down.

Modality

Each of the 12 Zodiac signs is also sorted into one of three modalities, which affects how they handle change. Some signs crave change like oxygen, while others would rather stay in the same place forever than make even the smallest adjustment to their routine.

Fixed

Taurus   Leo   Scorpio   Aquarius

Fixed signs are just that—fixed. They value steadiness above all things and require a lot of coaxing before they'll accept new ideas or ways of doing things. These stubborn signs are endlessly dependable—and frustrating.

Cardinal

Aries   Cancer   Libra   Capricorn

Cardinal signs will accept change, so long as it serves a purpose. These signs are action-oriented and love to be the initiators of change, particularly if it benefits them. Accepting changes brought on by others, however? That's another story...

Mutable

Gemini   Virgo   Sagittarius   Pisces

Mutable signs hate sameness and thrive off changes, big and small. While Virgo is all about making constant little tweaks in the hope of achieving perfection, Gemini is all about big, sweeping changes that upheave everything that came before. In either case, the person you talked to yesterday may be very different to the one you get today.

Opposing sign

The Zodiac is symbolized by a wheel and each sign has its opposite. While opposing signs tend to have very different ways of doing things, they are also typically complementary to each other and can make an amazing team. This is different from your sign's "mortal enemy," which is typically someone you'd have a very difficult time getting along with, even for short periods.

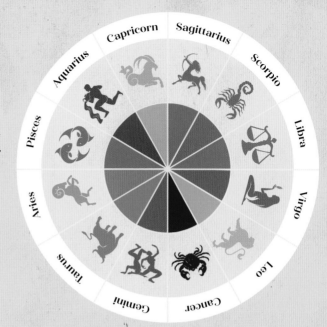

The big three

In astrology, your "big three" refers to the signs that make up your sun, moon, and rising sign in your birth chart (there are a lot of free birth chart calculators online). Your sun sign is the sign most closely identified with your sense of self, and it's the one you would answer with when someone asks, "What's your sign?" However, your moon and rising signs also have a big effect on your personality—sometimes for the worse.

Moon signs

Your moon sign represents your inner life. It rules over your feelings, emotions, and internal self. Basically, it's the version of you that only you know about because you rarely show it to the world.

Rising signs

By contrast, your rising sign is all about how the world sees you. It's your social personality and can tell you a lot about how you come across to other people.

Venus

In this book we've also included information about your Venus sign, which rules how you behave in your romantic relationships. If you're not connecting with the description of how your sun sign behaves in a relationship, it may be because you have a particularly pesky Venus sign at play.

Hello Aries...

Welcome to your burn book, Aries. Are you fuming yet? We're honestly surprised that a hothead like you would allow yourself to be roasted. But then again, you're so cocky you probably think we've got nothing negative to say. As per usual, you couldn't be more wrong. (Not that you'd ever admit it if you were.) Arrogant, insensitive, and impatient, you're the Zodiac's tantrum-throwing permanent toddler. On the bright side, at least you get to say you're number one...in anger, jealousy, and aggression. Your competitive side will love that.

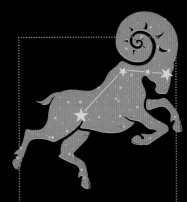

ZODIAC DATES
March 21–April 19

SYMBOL
Ram

RULER PLANET
Mars

ELEMENT
Fire

MODALITY
Cardinal

OPPOSING SIGN
Libra

MORTAL ENEMY
Taurus

PET PEEVES
Passive aggression,
coming in second, slow
walkers, waiting

5 NOTORIOUS ARIANS

Arians love to brag, so you may have heard them tout their connections to famous figures like Aretha Franklin and Céline Dion, but they might be better represented by these more infamous names:

1 **Giacomo Casanova (April 2, 1725):** Lothario who claimed to have slept with over 100 men and women across Europe. He also successfully escaped from prison on Halloween in 1756.

2 **Clyde Barrow (March 24, 1909):** Depression-era bank robber, murderer, and outlaw known for being one half of the infamous crime duo "Bonnie and Clyde."

3 **Lucrezia Borgia (April 18, 1480):** Femme fatale and daughter of Pope Alexander VI, Lucrezia has been accused of adultery, seduction, and poisoning, and is the subject of countless works of art.

4 **Butch Cassidy (April 13, 1866):** Bank and train robber, and leader of the "Wild Bunch" in the American Old West. His life was immortalized in the 1969 Academy Award-winning movie *Butch Cassidy and the Sundance Kid*.

5 **Vincent van Gogh (March 30, 1853):** Famous for works of art such as *Starry Night* but not in his lifetime. His self-portrait depicts the artist after cutting off his ear in a fit of rage.

Aries in a nutshell

Nice astrologers will call you confident, passionate, and an excellent leader—but we're not nice astrologers, so let's give it to you straight. Confident? More like self-obsessed. Passionate? More like hotheaded. An excellent leader? Only in the sense that you're so competitive you won't stop until you've reached the top (stepping on anyone who dares get in your way, of course).

I'd go on, but you've probably already run out of patience. Good on you for picking up a book, though. Brains over brawn isn't usually your strong suit. Just ask your friends, who are the most likely recipients of your half-baked, rage-fueled rants. They know anytime they take you out there's a high chance the night will end in a fight, usually with someone foolish enough to beat you at pool. We'd say it's a wonder they invite you anywhere, but they're probably too afraid of the epic meltdown that would ensue if you ever discovered they were hanging out without you.

Is this roast making you angry, Aries? Maybe you should take a moment to cool down before reading more. Or you could punch another hole in the wall.

HOTHEADED

Some may say you have a short fuse. We'd say your fuse is nonexistent. Aries are basically the Incredible Hulks of the Zodiac. You won't like them when they're angry. Aries can go from perfectly calm to rage-filled monster in an instant at even the most minor slight. Rams are happy to use their horns to butt heads with anyone and anything, but rarely stick around to deal with the consequences. Once they've calmed down, they move on like nothing ever happened. Their victims, on the other hand, are not so lucky.

ARROGANT

Pop star Demi Lovato once asked, "What's wrong with being confident?" Apparently, she's never met an Aries. What may seem like confidence at first, soon turns out to be arrogance for this sign. Aries are textbook narcissists, only able to see the world through their own narrow lens. Insensitive and inconsiderate, rams spend their life barreling ahead toward their goals, blissfully unaware of all the people they hurt along the way. Not that they would care if they knew. It's Aries' world and we're just living in it. If you can't get with it, it's best to just get out of the way.

COMPETITIVE

Aries is the first sign in the Zodiac, and as far as they're concerned they should be first in everything else too. This sign turns everything into a competition, and there's nothing they won't do to win. If they do, expect to hear them gloating about their accomplishment for years to come. And if they lose...honestly, we don't even want to think about it. Just ask their siblings why they can't even hear the words "family game night" without running for cover. This argumentative sign will never back down or admit when they're wrong, even if the right answer is staring them in the face. Probably why they make such good politicians.

Aries placements

Got Aries elsewhere in your chart? Then you've got a problem. This Mars-ruled sign has a way of dominating the personality of anyone it does business with. And you thought your sun sign was the problem...

MOON IN ARIES

Your moon sign represents your subconscious. If your moon is in Aries, that means your subconscious is impatient, flaky, and trigger-happy. If you've always wondered why you have a hard time sitting still for a meditation or spend hours of your day imagining arguments with strangers, this is why. No wonder you can't stand being alone with your thoughts. They're kind of unbearable.

ARIES RISING

Your rising sign represents how the world sees you, so I regret to inform you that an Aries rising means the world sees you as an aggressive, pushy extrovert with a hair-trigger temper. It's probably why so many invitations have gotten "lost in the mail." Nobody wants a wild card at their birthday party, especially one who might start throwing punches.

VENUS IN ARIES

Just because you're not an Aries sun sign, doesn't mean you're safe from getting burned. Time to meet the Zodiac's resident f'boy: the Aries Venus. Someone with their Venus in Aries thrives in high-conflict relationships. Though "relationships" may be too strong of a word. Fiercely independent, Aries Venuses will resist settling down until the bitter end, preferring to play the field rather than risk getting played themselves. They'll swipe on new matches all day, but when it comes time to meeting up, they go dark. Hopefully they have a library card, because they've been leaving a lot of people on read.

Aries in love

Aries' romantic motto is simple: here today, gone tomorrow. This passion-fueled sign is all about the chase, and rarely wants to stick it out for the long haul. A casual look at their romantic history will unearth a slew of hurt feelings and bitter resentments. Not that Aries cares. They're already onto their next conquest—I mean—relationship.

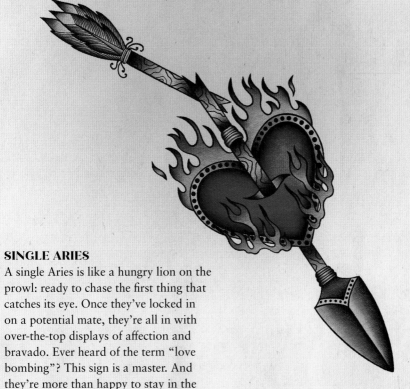

SINGLE ARIES

A single Aries is like a hungry lion on the prowl: ready to chase the first thing that catches its eye. Once they've locked in on a potential mate, they're all in with over-the-top displays of affection and bravado. Ever heard of the term "love bombing"? This sign is a master. And they're more than happy to stay in the "what are we?" phase of a relationship forever rather than make a commitment. Their notch-on-the-bedpost mindset lends itself well to a series of passionate flings that burn hot in the moment, but grow cold the moment their partner starts to catch feelings. Even worse, despite the fact that this love-'em-and-leave-'em sign isn't looking for anything serious, they also can't handle rejection. As far as Aries is concerned, they're the ones who should be doing the rejecting—usually just a matter of moments after using the "L" word for the first time.

ARIES IN A RELATIONSHIP

Think you've gotten an Aries to commit? Are you sure about that? This sign's wandering eye is legendary, and they'll always be more attracted to potential affairs over true partnership. Ever the hypocrite, this sign is also incredibly jealous and probably only committed to their partner to make sure no one else can have them. This impulsive sign is not afraid to go through a partner's phone, and loses their cool at anyone who dares show their partner interest (or even just basic pleasantries). Because of this, Aries' relationships tend to be drama-filled messes that blow up into acrimonious splits. In short? This sign is a divorce lawyer's dream.

Most compatible

Aries + Gemini

Fire and air make an explosive pair with these two. Gemini's constant changeability and go-with-the-flow attitude means Aries will never be bored, and their fire will always be stoked by Gemini's constant gusts of energy and new ideas. On the flip side, Gemini will love the drama that their hot-headed Aries partner brings, and doesn't take their constant conflict too seriously. In fact, they find it kind of funny. Get these two on a reality show ASAP.

Least compatible

Aries + Aries

This is a match made in the fiery pits of hell. We've already talked about Aries' infamous competitive streak, so when two rams get together they can't help but butt heads trying to one-up each other at every turn. In arguments, neither side will ever back down. These explosive fights inevitably lead to explosive making-up sessions, much to the chagrin of the neighbors, who are sick of hearing *everything* through the walls. An Aries-on-Aries match may go on forever as the two become stuck in a toxic loop of winning each other over just to break up (loudly, and in public) all over again. They're the epitome of the idea that just because a relationship can last, doesn't mean it should.

Aries + Virgo

When it comes to this pair, opposites attract… and then repel each other. Explosive anger meets slow boiling rage with these two. While Aries is all fire and in-the-moment passion, Virgo is a slow burn. Virgos prefer to lay a solid foundation, prizing stability and consistency above flights of fancy and spontaneous connection. Unfortunately for Aries, flights of fancy are kind of their whole deal. The patience required to bag a Virgo is enough to drive any Aries mad, and the more rams try to barrel ahead with over-the-top gestures and professions of love, the more a Virgo is likely to raise their guard. Ultimately, these two are better off as friends. Or even more likely, as frenemies.

Aries + Cancer

Aries and Cancer go together about as well as you'd expect for fire and water. Insensitive Aries will find themselves constantly at odds with emotional Cancer, a sign that's best known for taking everything very personally. But it's trust issues that will ultimately bring this match down. Cancer will be completely unable to deal with Aries' wandering eye, and unempathetic Aries will be totally unable (and unwilling) to stop. Cancer's need to discuss their feelings douses cold water on Aries' passion. While Aries wants nothing more than to move on, Cancer only feels safe if they can stay put and process. In the end, they should do themselves a favor and stay away from each other.

ARIES AT WORK

A moment of silence for all your coworkers, Aries. We don't envy them. You're not sure why you're always butting heads. All your coworkers have to do is agree with everything you say, shower you with constant praise, and never push back. You have a much easier time getting along with (aka sucking up to) your boss, but that's only to mask the fact that you spend every waking moment plotting how you can steal their job. Unfortunately for you, your big plans always lack follow-through. Coworkers know not to go to you for help or trust you with their ideas—you'll be at the front of the boardroom presenting them as your own by the end of the week. Even worse, you're that coworker who talks loudly in the common areas, microwaves fish, and flies off the handle if anyone dares to complain.

ARIES IN THE FAMILY

If anyone knows how to speak to your hotheaded, competitive side, it's your own family members. You're the one who can't get through a holiday meal without a fight, and you certainly can't get through a simple game of Monopoly without flipping the board over at least once. Even worse is when you win, which will lead to days of non-stop gloating. Siblings, cousins, and basically any family member in your age bracket knows better than to tell grandma about their accomplishments when Aries is around. They just can't help but hijack the conversation to talk about how they did it bigger and better, whether that's actually true or not. Relationships with parents are equally fraught, as Aries' problems with authority are legendary. Nobody can tell them what to do, even their legal guardian. Daddy issues abound with this sign, as they are pathologically driven to supersede the accomplishments of their father, while also desperately seeking his praise and attention. Frankly, you make the antics of the *Succession* siblings look like child's play.

ARIES AT HOME

Does a person live here, or a tornado? The Aries home is defined by one thing: mess. Aries tear through their living space like a whirlwind, and cannot be bothered to put anything back where it belongs. Unworn outfits lay discarded on the floor, half-drunk water glasses stay out until they leave a stain (of course, Aries forgot a coaster), and chaos reigns supreme in the Aries home. As a result, you're constantly losing important items like your glasses, keys, and wallet, leading to fits of rage and more than a few holes punched into the wall. By now you probably have a locksmith on speed dial. Roommates know better than to ask you to lend a hand with the dishes or pick up your old takeout lest they start World War Three. Or is it World War Six? That's why living alone tends to work best for rams. You love nothing more than to start a DIY project, but can never seem to finish them, meaning half-built shelves and haphazardly painted walls abound. You may see no problem with it, but guests and— ahem—overnight visitors will be horrified at the chaos. Best to get a hotel.

ARIES AND TRAVEL

You know those people at the airport who hold up the security line because they didn't take out their ID, left their laptop in their bag, have a pocket full of random items, and somehow managed to leave multiple unauthorized liquids in their carry-on? That's Aries. Aries are basically allergic to planning, meaning when they travel, it is always by the seat of their pants. They're the ones rushing to their gate at the very last minute with a bag full of random crap they threw together last night (meaning they're bound to have left something really important behind.) Worse yet, they make their lack of planning everybody else's problem, and are not opposed to getting in a fight with the gate agent just because a flight dared leave without them. Once they arrive at their destination, they dominate group activities by refusing to compromise on what to eat, what sights to see, and when to head back to the hotel. They're the tourist that shows up in a foreign country and expects the locals to speak their language, accept their currency, and generally cater to their every whim. Basically, they're a viral airport freakout video just waiting to happen.

The two sides of Aries

Aries is considered one of the more masculine signs in the Zodiac (hence the testosterone-fueled fits of rage), but all Aries have both a dark masculine and dark feminine side to them. Regardless of gender identity, which ram you get will depend on what side of the bed they woke up on that day. Here are the different (though still irrationally angry) rams you may have to contend with on a given day, or some toxic combination of the two.

ARIES DARK MASCULINE

When an Aries is situated in their dark masculine side, they are stubborn, impulsive, insensitive, and physically aggressive. When an Aries is operating on a hair trigger and seems to be out looking for a fight, they're situated in their dark masculine. Best to steer clear of rams on these days. Unless you want to end up with a black eye.

ARIES DARK FEMININE

When an Aries is getting in touch with their dark feminine side, they become self-obsessed, hypercompetitive, flaky, and bulldozing. These are the days when they can't feel satisfied unless all eyes are on them, particularly when it comes to romantic prospects. We'd tell you to avoid them on these days as well, but the more you avoid them, the more they'll vie for your attention. Best to just shower them with the praise they crave and move on with your day.

Aries cusp

ARIES–TAURUS CUSP
(APRIL 17–APRIL 23)

Angry *and* dull? Aren't you a catch. Like most cusps, you're
dominated by the personality of the star sign you fall within (as
if Aries would have it any other way), but the bull was able to
muscle its way in there a little bit. This means that while you
may have a tiny bit of Taurus's work ethic, you still get bored
easily and will drop a project the moment you're challenged
or face the slightest inconvenience. Pushy, stubborn, and
controlling, you've got all of Aries' fire but lack the
spark that makes them fun. It truly is
the worst of both worlds.

Hello Taurus...

For someone so materialistic, you sure are dull. I'll give you a second to catch up to what I'm saying here. You're not exactly known for being quick-witted. Fueled by resentment and an insatiable love of money, you put the "bull" in bully in the most boring, average way possible. Some may call you reliable, but the rest of us know the truth: you're stuck in a rut. And you've got nobody to blame for it but yourself.

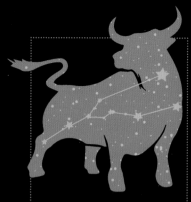

ZODIAC DATES
April 20–May 20

SYMBOL
Bull

RULER PLANET
Venus

ELEMENT
Earth

MODALITY
Fixed

OPPOSING SIGN
Scorpio

MORTAL ENEMY
Gemini

PET PEEVES
Late people, bland food, being rushed, sudden changes

5 NOTORIOUS TAUREANS

Sure, Taureans love to discuss how they share a star sign with the likes of William Shakespeare and Janet Jackson, but what about the darker branches of the Taurus family tree? Here are five Taureans who exemplify the worst of this star sign:

1 **Maximilien Robespierre (May 6, 1758):** Pivotal to the "Reign of Terror" during the French Revolution in which political opponents were guillotined for treason with Taurean efficiency.

2 **Catherine the Great (May 2, 1729):** Russian Empress who had her husband murdered to take power. An apocryphal story claimed she once had sexual relations with a horse.

3 **Robert Oppenheimer (April 22, 1904):** American theoretical physicist known as the "father of the atomic bomb" for his role in developing the first nuclear weapons.

4 **Sid Vicious (May 10, 1957):** Punk musician and bassist for the Sex Pistols, Vicious was accused of killing his partner Nancy Spungeon and died shortly thereafter, claiming they'd had a "death pact" to never live apart.

5 **Tsar Nicholas II (May 18, 1868):** Last Russian tsar whose death at the hands of the Bolsheviks marked the start of the 1917 Russian Revolution.

Taurus in a nutshell

Most astrology books will tell you how hardworking you are. They'll tell you how much you love comfort, sensory pleasures, and life's finer things. We'll tell you that you're a stubborn Scrooge, if Scrooge was too stuck-in-a-rut to even consider joining the three ghosts at Christmas. Your obsession with your own comfort blocks out all other concerns, meaning you are that friend who everyone knows will take way more than their fair share of the appetizers during dinner at the too-expensive restaurant you insisted on attending. As for temperament, it's the worst of both worlds for you, Taurus. Too nonconfrontational to get your problems solved, but too judgmental to let it go. You're opinionated, even when the opinion is dull and boring. Sure, you may have a nice house and a fancy car, but what are they worth if your guests are too bored to enjoy it with you?

STUBBORN

Even the most rosy astrological breakdowns will talk about your stubbornness, bull, but let's really talk about it. You hate change, even if it's minor or will make things better in the long run, which is why you look around year after year and find yourself in the exact same place you were when you started. Your inability to be flexible makes you rut-bound, plus you're too opinionated and overbearing to just let others live their lives around you. People can feel the judgment, and they stay far, far away. No wonder you always see bulls in a pen all by themselves. Their "leave me alone" signals are received loud and clear.

MATERIALISTIC

Sure, you got the sharing lesson in preschool, Taurus, but it never really stuck. As one of the most materialistic signs of the Zodiac, your money-and-status obsession borders on tacky. Just because something is expensive, doesn't mean it's actually nice, but there's no use explaining that to you, Taurus. You're that person who needs name-brand everything to feel secure, even if your friends cringe at the sight of the matching Louis Vuitton purse and wallet you take out to performatively pay for everyone's food. It may seem like a nice gesture, but everyone knows your "generosity" is rooted in jealousy and petty resentments. Nobody missed the fact that your ostentatious display of wealth came at the exact same time as Sharon's promotion. You're just not slick enough to pull off being a sneak.

BORING

Yaaaawwwwnnnn—that's my impression of anyone in your presence for more than five minutes, Taurus. Like the bovine you're named for, you're dull, plodding, and frankly boring to be around. Your conservative, traditional values mean there's no chance for surprises with you. Just the same old field, eating the same old grass, day after day. You're the friend who takes the same tacky resort vacation every year and models their wedding after Queen Victoria. Boring!

Taurus placements

While the Taurus sun sign is our focus here, having Taurus as any of your "big three" placements is probably the reason you find yourself stuck in the mud. This slow-moving, stubborn sign has a way of halting the progress of anything in its path.

MOON IN TAURUS

Your moon sign represents your subconscious mind, meaning that your mind is subconsciously sex-obsessed, materialistic, and adverse to change. If you find yourself thinking about the same two things over and over (usually sex or money), your Taurus moon is probably why. We'd tell you to break the cycle, but staying stuck in a loop is kind of Taurus's whole deal.

TAURUS RISING

Your rising sign dictates how the world sees you, and most importantly the first impression you give. So what first impression does a Taurus rising give? A resounding "bleh." Thoroughly unremarkable, a Taurus rising will have to fight to show off their fun side. Maybe on the second impression...if there is one.

VENUS IN TAURUS

Those with a Venus in Taurus will say they're looking for a partner that can provide stability and comfort. Those of us who can read between the lines will say they're looking for a meal ticket. The ultimate gold digger, Taurus Venuses will leverage their sexuality to move up in the world and find a partner who can afford to give them a life of luxury. Their partners can test this theory by uttering the word "prenup" and seeing how fast their beloved sees red.

Taurus in love

Some astrology books will say that the sensual Taurus is something of a stallion in the sack. They may even call you a sex god. We'd call you a sex robot. While you may be methodically pleasing both yourself and your partner with your time-tested moves, Taurus lacks the ability to connect emotionally with their lovers. Once the deed is done, conversation fizzles and Taurus's partners consistently find they have nothing to talk about. Unless, of course, they bring up work, in which case Taurus will drone on and on about the minutiae of their career without any acknowledgment that their partner is bored to tears, or asking them a single question in return.

SINGLE TAURUS

Are you a single Taurus wondering why you're still alone? Probably because you don't play well with others. Taurus wants everything done exactly their way, and will spend their entire life searching for a carbon copy of themselves. This stubborn sign will hold their ground on anything and everything, from how to raise kids to where to go out to eat on a Friday night. They'd rather let a promising partnership fall apart than let go of control, which is why they often do. Their superior lovemaking skills mean Taurus can spend a lifetime hopping from bed to bed, but a deeper connection will elude them until they learn to compromise.

TAURUS IN A RELATIONSHIP

Want to know how to get Taurus to commit? Just stick around. Once a Taurus has established a routine, they'd rather die than upend it. Long-suffering Taureans will stay in a toxic, spark-less relationship for their entire lives simply because they don't want to deal with all the change that comes with a breakup. Anyone unlucky enough to need to shake off their Taurus lover will find the task exceptionally hard, as stubborn bulls will just keep plodding their way back to your door (or into your DMs) for eternity rather than take on the task of moving on.

Most compatible

Taurus + Taurus

Is it any surprise that the best match for Taurus is...another Taurus? This stubborn sign refuses to relent on anything and absolutely hates change, so their perfect partner is someone who sees the world through their same (boring, unoriginal) lens. A Taurus-on-Taurus match will spend their days sitting on the same couch, eating the same food, and having the selfsame conversation over and over again in perfect bliss.

Least compatible

Taurus + Sagittarius

Sagittarius loves spontaneity, change, and a life of constant excitement. See the problem? While the sexual prowess of Taurus may provide the initial excitement Sagittarius needs, it's their lack of stamina outside of the bedroom that will spell doom for this couple. While Taurus loves nothing more than a night in on the couch, Sagittarius thrives off adventure and trying new things. It won't be long before fiery archers move on from their earth-bound lovers, even if Taurus never does.

Taurus + Gemini

Gemini is an air sign that lives life flying high above the clouds. Taurus is an earth sign that prefers to stay stuck-in-the mud. To keep a Gemini's attention, a partner will need to provide a constant stream of intellectually stimulating conversation. Taurus would rather talk about the weather…again. The mismatch here is so stark that this pairing is unlikely to make it past the first date, which will most likely be spent in awkward silence. At least the dinner was good.

Taurus + Leo

A love of materialism will draw these two together, and they may make quite the pretty pair, but their stubbornness will inevitably drive them apart. Both of these signs live by the motto "it's my way or the highway," and will absolutely refuse to budge when their worldviews don't align. This pair may initially dazzle each other with their high-end fashion sense and love of fine dining, but as soon as an issue arises where they'll have to compromise, it's splitsville for these two.

TAURUS AT WORK

Any Taurus who has investigated their sun sign at all will have heard that they're hardworking and dependable. And that's true! To a fault. At work, Taurus is that long-suffering colleague who takes on every task and completes it perfectly, but somehow never seems to move up in the world. Day after day, year after year, Taurus can be found at the same desk, eating the same lunch, plodding away. They may feel anger watching all of their younger, less hardworking colleagues rise in the ranks around them, but it's never enough to actually get them to do something about it. They'll stay in a toxic workplace for years rather than quit and change up their routine, even as they endure the humiliation of watching their former intern suddenly become their boss. Taurus loves nothing more than to be a cog in the corporate machine, and will spend their entire life quietly completing their tasks until the day comes for their tepid, lackluster retirement party—or they simply drop dead at their desk.

TAURUS IN THE FAMILY

On the one hand, a Taurus family member often serves as the root of the family tree thanks to their steady dependability and ability to cook a holiday meal. On the other hand, this tradition-obsessed sign will throw a fit at any hint of change, and cannot help but hold family members to their obsessive and conservative standards. Any attempt to change up the dynamic will be met by fierce resistance from Taurus, who simply cannot imagine why someone would want to live a life that's different from their own. They're the family members who always find faults with their sibling's new partner and can't seem to wrap their head around their artsy cousin's "alternative" lifestyle. Whenever family events come around, Taurus will throw their weight around to make sure everything is planned to their standards, which usually means doing things the exact same way they've been done since their great-great-grandma's days. Vegetarian cousin wants to introduce some new dishes to the holiday table? Get ready for Taurus to fight, push, and pout every step of the way. Mess with the bull, get the horns. Particularly when it comes to the menu.

TAURUS AT HOME

A Taurus's home is truly their castle, and they're happy to raise the gates and stay locked inside for the rest of their days. Home is where Taurus stores all their precious material possessions, so it's no wonder they take interior decorating very, very seriously. Much like with their wardrobe, Taurus has to have name-brand everything. They'll spend hours meticulously decorating their space, and then proceed to never change it, regardless of whether their wallpaper is outdated or carpeting has fallen out of vogue. Houseguests will find that bulls have curated a lovely, comfortable home for themselves...and only themselves. Guests—even ones who pay for room and board—had best conform to Taurus's exacting standards, or feel their host's wrath. Each item has its place and proper decorum must be observed while walking a Taurus's hallowed halls. Dinner guests should brush up on their manners before taking a seat at the Taurus table. Host gifts are expected, and they'll also be judged to Taurus's strict rules. Bring a bottle of wine worth less than $20 and don't expect an invitation back.

TAURUS AND TRAVEL

When a Taurus does decide to venture outside the home, they want to do it exactly their way, which is usually both expensive and unadventurous. They go into a vacation with every hour of the day planned, and cannot abide changes to the itinerary. Unexpected flight delays or changes to the plan will lead to a full-on meltdown, as will basic travel mishaps like a bout of jet lag or a toothbrush left at home. A Taurus is never going to want to go off the beaten path to check out an unmarked local haunt or take a risk on a cheap train or hostel. They'd much rather plod along the same path of millions of other tourists before them, staying in the same hotel chain where they've been accruing travel points for years. By the end of the trip, a Taurus will be telling everyone in their vicinity how much they cannot wait to get home, with a bagful of chintzy souvenirs and photos of themselves pretending to hold up the Eiffel Tower in tow.

The two sides of Taurus

Taurus is one of the feminine signs of the Zodiac, but all Taureans have both a dark masculine and dark feminine side. Regardless of gender identity, which bull you get will depend on a number of factors like stress level, proximity to home, and whether or not they got a good night's sleep. Sometimes it can feel like a simple roll of the dice. Here are the two poles of the Taurus personality, each one as stubborn and unyielding as the last.

TAURUS DARK MASCULINE

When Taurus is falling on the masculine side, they become a work-obsessed, sex-obsessed drone. Try to engage them on a topic other than work, and you'll find them staring blankly in response, or getting angry that you interrupted their daily spreadsheet analysis. The only thing that might pull them away from the monotony of the office are offers of food or sex, which will ultimately culminate in the bull rolling over to fall asleep without a word—unless you count loud, methodical snores as conversation.

TAURUS DARK FEMININE

When a Taurus is feeling particularly feminine, their exacting, judgmental side comes to the forefront. They become obsessive in their home life, and cannot help but try to bully family and loved ones into living life the way they think is best. Like the stepmom from hell, they impose their obsessive materialism on everyone around them and are unrelenting in their expectations of manners and decorum. Elbows off the table, you lout!

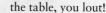

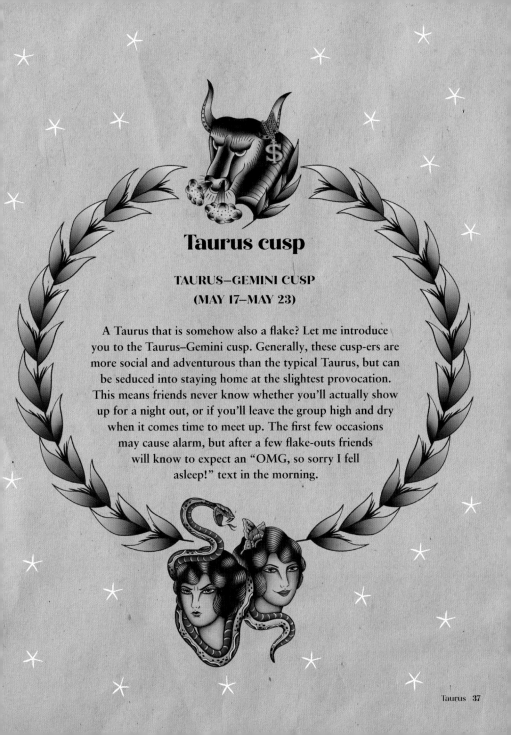

Taurus cusp

TAURUS–GEMINI CUSP
(MAY 17–MAY 23)

A Taurus that is somehow also a flake? Let me introduce you to the Taurus–Gemini cusp. Generally, these cusp-ers are more social and adventurous than the typical Taurus, but can be seduced into staying home at the slightest provocation. This means friends never know whether you'll actually show up for a night out, or if you'll leave the group high and dry when it comes time to meet up. The first few occasions may cause alarm, but after a few flake-outs friends will know to expect an "OMG, so sorry I fell asleep!" text in the morning.

Hello Gemini...

We're honestly surprised you could pay attention to one book long enough to make it this far. Though, let's be honest, you probably just skipped right to your own chapter. You are the main character of the universe, after all. You may have fooled the rest of the world into thinking you're smart by knowing a little bit about everything, but we know the truth. You're the epitome of the phrase "jack of all trades, master of none." Once somebody decides to dig deeper, your sparkly personality loses its shine faster than you lose interest in a romantic partner—or five.

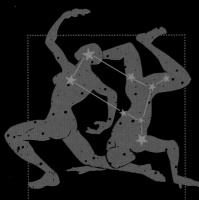

DATES
May 21–June 20

SYMBOL
Twins

RULER PLANET
Mercury

ELEMENT
Air

MODALITY
Mutable

OPPOSING SIGN
Sagittarius

MORTAL ENEMY
Other Geminis

PET PEEVES
Boring
conversations,
serious people,
fixed schedules,
being interrupted

5 NOTORIOUS GEMINIS

Movie stars, dictators, and philanderers—Geminis can count them all in their illustrious ranks. It would honestly be easier for us to create a list of famous Geminis who aren't in some way notorious, but here's a sampling of just five:

1 **Marilyn Monroe (June 1, 1926):** Beautiful actress and sex symbol of Hollywood's Golden Age, Marilyn's magnetic sexuality led to multiple high-profile marriages and affairs.

2 **Marquis de Sade (June 2, 1740):** French nobleman and philosopher whose sexually graphic novels gave rise to the term "sadism."

3 **Errol Flynn (June 20, 1909):** Hollywood heartthrob, womanizer, and on-screen swashbuckler, Flynn is infamous for a life of hard drinking, failed marriages, and legal troubles.

4 **Henry Hill (June 11, 1943):** American mobster whose life of crime at the behest of the Lucchese crime family in New York City inspired Martin Scorcese's 1990 movie *Goodfellas*.

5 **Wallis Simpson (June 19, 1896):** American divorcee, lover, and wife of King Edward VIII. Their relationship eventually led to Edward's abdication from the throne. The pair went on to live in exile in France and were said to have developed Nazi ties.

Gemini in a nutshell

You've spent your whole life being praised for your wit and intellect, but we're done with all that. Gossipy, devious, and thoroughly unreliable, Gemini draws people in only to leave them disappointed (and potentially heartbroken) just a short while later. Consummate con artists, Geminis will steal candy from a baby only to decide they don't actually want candy and toss it in the trash a moment later.

Think a Gemini is your friend? Not for long. Gemini friendships may burn bright, but they also burn out quickly, as this air-headed sign is always looking for the next best thing. As a Mercury-ruled sign, you probably see yourself as a top-notch conversationalist. In reality, you dominate the dialogue by waxing poetic about your favorite topics while simultaneously looking over your conversation partner's shoulder to see if someone cooler has come along. A roguish social climber, you tend to bring a "use-'em-and-lose-'em" mentality to your friendships, and your love of gossip means you've probably made more than a few enemies on your way to the top.

UNRELIABLE

What's the worst way to get a Gemini to do something? Ask them to do it. The ultimate commitment-phobe, Geminis are pathologically incapable of keeping their word. In fact, the more firm a commitment they make, the less likely they are to actually follow through. You'd much rather spend your life chasing the latest shiny object than be bothered with trivial things like "keeping your word." Coworkers know better than to expect you'll meet important deadlines, and friends are used to having you flake out on important events like birthdays, baby showers, and engagement parties. To be honest, they're not even sure you'll show up to your own wedding.

TWO-FACED

Geminis are known as "the Twins," so is it any wonder they tend to have two faces? Geminis love gossip, and their only loyalty is to their ability to tell a good story. Loved ones learn quickly not to share a juicy secret with you, as it'll be plastered across several group chats by morning. Forever the charmer, Geminis will make a person feel as if they're the best of friends when they're in conversation, then turn around and trash-talk them to whoever will listen as soon as they leave the room. You may be fun to hang out with at a party or a night out on the town, but your shifty sign will never actually show up for a friend when the going gets tough for them—unless you need fodder for your ever-expanding rotation of party stories, that is.

IMMATURE

Whether they're eight or eighty, Geminis spend their whole life searching for the fountain of youth and only finding Botox. Forever a slave to trends and fads, Gemini lives suspended in a state of arrested development. This restless, fickle-minded sign hates to be tied down by "adult" expectations like showing up to work on time or paying the bills. You may try to spin being a "child at heart" as a good thing, but those closest to you will quickly grow tired of your silly antics and inability to take life seriously. The childishness often gives way to full-on temper tantrums when you're called to account for your bad behavior. This behavior may have worked in elementary school, but as you grow older you'll find more and more people are willing to simply leave you in the sandbox.

Gemini placements

The Gemini sun sign may be the main focus in this chapter, but having the Twins as any of your "big three" means you may find yourself at the mercy of their flaky, unpredictable ways. This verbose sign is known for dominating conversations...and any birth chart where it may appear.

GEMINI RISING

Tell people about your Gemini rising sign, and they might respond by saying that's why the world sees you as witty and intelligent. What they're not saying is that they also see you as a shallow social climber who's not to be trusted. You've probably spent your whole life hearing about your "sparkling personality," but most people also get the impression that your shine and substance do not go hand in hand.

MOON IN GEMINI

Can't seem to settle your thoughts? Meditation leaving you frustrated and restless? You can thank your Gemini moon, which is characterized by a deep and abiding fear of boredom. With their head perpetually in the clouds, Gemini moons find it nearly impossible to live in the present. They'd rather spend their life losing themselves in elaborate fantasies, usually about world domination. Unfortunately however, you need self-discipline for that.

VENUS IN GEMINI

Got your Venus in Gemini? No wonder you can't commit. You're a master at getting potential partners interested, but your heart's teeny-tiny attention span means you're always battling your own wandering eye. Gemini Venuses are perpetually awash with romantic possibilities, meaning they always have someone waiting in the wings when their current relationship fizzles out. These placements love the start of relationships—when everything is fun and carefree—but will run the moment the romance starts to turn serious or their partner wants to impose expectations.

Gemini in love

We'll start with the good stuff, Gemini. You're a really good flirt. Like, really good. Don't believe us? Just ask one of the multiple partners you're probably juggling as we speak. Your double-crossing sign is all flirt and no follow-through, meaning you have no problem maintaining multiple romantic partners—or professing love to them all. Once it comes time to actually defining the relationship, suddenly your sign has nothing to say. What's that, Gemini? Commitment got your tongue?

SINGLE GEMINI

In many ways, a single Gemini is a happy Gemini. This air sign hates to be tied down, and would much prefer to float from fling to fling than deal with someone else's suffocating relationship standards. As a master communicator, you have no problem lingering in the "texting phase" of a relationship and never actually meeting up for a date. In fact, the will-they-won't-they of flirting is your favorite part of the process. Once things move from the realm of "what ifs?" you start getting bored. And once you start getting bored, you quickly make your exit. The ultimate player, Gemini has no problem charming the pants off someone one night, only to forget about them by morning. No wonder so many people have blocked you on the apps.

GEMINI IN A RELATIONSHIP

As the Zodiac's ultimate commitment-phobe, you may technically agree to be in a relationship, but you'll never truly settle down. Even when partnered up, you prefer to keep your options open, and any beau of yours will have to be okay with your penchant for flirting with anything that moves. Or not! It doesn't bother Gemini. In fact, you prefer a relationship in which a constant cycle of making up and breaking up is just part of the deal. It helps to keep things interesting—and "interesting" is Gemini's *raison d'être*. If you do settle down over the long term, it'll probably be with someone whose wealth and status helps to elevate your own. All the better for when you take half and run.

Most compatible

Gemini + Aquarius

Gemini's ultimate match is Aquarius. As a fellow air sign, Aquarius is too caught up in their own lofty ideals to try to pull Gemini back to earth, and their status as the Zodiac's resident "weirdo" means they'll always keep the Twins on their toes. This heady sign is happy to keep things intellectual rather than emotional, and the two can spend hours exchanging ideas about everything under the sun. Aquarius's emotional distance is perfect for Gemini, as they'll never get attached enough to be hurt by Gemini's wandering eye or complete inability to commit. In fact, they may not even notice when Gemini is gone.

Least compatible

Gemini + Capricorn

Earth-bound Capricorns are way too frigid and serious for light-hearted Gemini, and will quickly leave them feeling suffocated and restrained: two emotions the Twins simply cannot abide. Capricorn is all about commitment, which is something Gemini will never be able to provide. Even worse, Capricorns remember every promise and will expect Geminis to stick to what they say—a nearly impossible task for a sign whose moods change with the time of day.

Gemini + Sagittarius

This air and fire pairing is bound to be explosive. At first, they'll be drawn to each other's fun-loving lifestyles and ability to match wits. Plus, Sagittarius's recklessness will provide Gemini with the sense of adventure they crave. Unfortunately, adventure also spells danger for these two, as they'll egg each other on and inflame each other's worst tendencies. They could end up stuck in the makeup-and-breakup cycle that Gemini craves, but ultimately Sagittarius's tendency to call Gemini out when they're wrong will spell the end for this combustible couple.

Gemini + Taurus

Sensual, material Taurus may be able to attract a Gemini with their brand-name clothes and reputation for being good in the sack, but simply put, Taurus is way too dull to keep Gemini around for more than an evening. Taurus's total disinterest in intellectual pursuits will leave Gemini bored to tears the moment their initial attraction fades. As soon as the conversation lulls—usually moments after the two have finished doing the deed—Gemini will find themselves making any excuse to get out of Taurus's bed. Not that Taurus minds. They have work in the morning.

GEMINI AT WORK

A job? Gemini? Not for long. Your sign is not one for steady employment. Sure, your mastery of the skill of "faking it till you make it" means you often wow during the interview stage, but you quickly lose interest and disappoint your boss once it comes to actually doing the job you've been hired for. Similarly, you'll probably dazzle your coworkers with your water-cooler chitchat, but that great first impression will quickly fade once they learn about your real job: purveyor of office gossip. Once a Gemini finds a job they actually do like, their devious nature will kick into high gear and they'll double-cross and manipulate anyone they can to climb the ladder. If only you could put some of that energy into doing your actual job. But that would be way too boring for Gemini, who needs constant stimuli to stop from jumping out of their skin. This sign is more suited to a "non-traditional" job—con artist, influencer, and double agent come to mind.

GEMINI AT HOME

Given your long history of ghosting romantic partners, it's kind of fitting that your home looks like nobody's lived there in years. Geminis hate to sit still and rarely spend their waking hours at home, meaning their living space tends to look more like a hostel than a home. If Gemini does manage to decorate, their interior design philosophy can usually be described as…incoherent. Your preferred décor usually consists of an assortment of shiny objects that you've collected on your travels randomly scattered across haphazardly installed shelves. These magpie-like tendencies can make living with Gemini a nightmare, as housemates never know when they'll come home to another musty furniture item (or even a live animal) that Gemini has pulled off the street to care for.

GEMINI IN THE FAMILY

No matter where you actually fall in the birth order, you always want to be the baby. And what Gemini wants, Gemini gets. Especially since you know exactly what to say to charm the pants off grandma while simultaneously putting in the bare minimum at birthdays, holidays, and other important family events. Is your presence not present enough? Gemini loves to roll up to the family reunion and collect accolades for their own (heavily embellished) accomplishments, while also retaining almost nothing about what everyone else has been up to. Unless, of course, there's some juicy gossip. You're always the first to blast the family business far and wide so long as it makes for a good story, and your siblings will probably go to their grave waiting for an apology for that time you told the whole school about their little bed-wetting problem. As you grow older, the younger generation will love your silly "fun aunt" antics, but adult family members know better than to call you for babysitting duty unless they want to come home to a freaked-out kiddo (thanks to the R-rated scary movie you let them watch) who's hopped up on candy (in place of dinner) and up way past their bedtime (what bedtime?). Ultimately, you're happy to accept a perpetual seat at the kids' table rather than deal with all the responsibilities that come with joining the adults.

GEMINI AND TRAVEL

On the one hand, you love the idea of travel. On the other, you hate doing the things that are required to make travel happen like booking flights, finding a hotel, or—worst of all—packing a bag. In theory, your love of adventure should lend itself to being a good travel partner, but in practice you become immediately overwhelmed by all the possibilities your destination holds, while also refusing to be tied down by things like "hotel checkout times" and "dinner reservations." Rather than following a prescribed plan, you'd rather wander the streets of your new locale and just see what happens. As a result, you'll often leave without having seen any of the sites your destination is famous for but with at least two new international lovers who think they are your one true love.

The two sides of Gemini

Gemini is considered one of the masculine signs in the Zodiac, but all Geminis have dark masculine and dark feminine tendencies within them. No matter where you fall on the gender spectrum, you may find yourself flipping between either of these two versions of Gemini on any given day. Actually, let's be honest, you may find yourself flipping between the two even within the same hour. They don't call you "the Twins" for nothing, do they?

GEMINI DARK MASCULINE

Reckless. Thrill-seeking. Player. All three adjectives can be used to describe a Gemini who is getting in touch with their masculine side. When they are in touch with their dark masculine, Geminis have an intense desire to show off. They become braggarts who absolutely must be the smartest person in any room they enter. And if someone arrives who threatens their intellectual dominance? Get ready to start swinging.

GEMINI DARK FEMININE

When a Gemini is in touch with their dark feminine they become a charming heartbreaker and incorrigible flirt. The ultimate scammer, these femme fatales have no problem using their charms to get ahead and get what they want, then dip as soon as things start to get serious— or the check arrives. Paying the bill? Gemini? Not a chance.

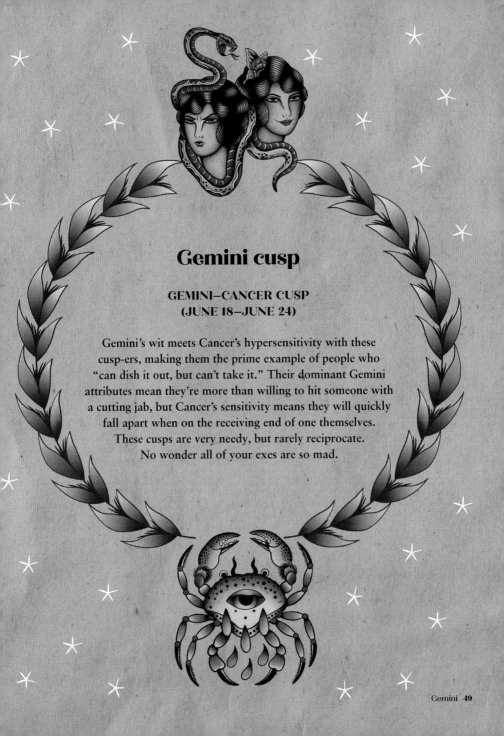

Gemini cusp

GEMINI–CANCER CUSP
(JUNE 18–JUNE 24)

Gemini's wit meets Cancer's hypersensitivity with these
cusp-ers, making them the prime example of people who
"can dish it out, but can't take it." Their dominant Gemini
attributes mean they're more than willing to hit someone with
a cutting jab, but Cancer's sensitivity means they will quickly
fall apart when on the receiving end of one themselves.
These cusps are very needy, but rarely reciprocate.
No wonder all of your exes are so mad.

Hello Cancer...

It's your turn to get roasted Cancer—*and* you're already crying. No surprises there.
Your watery, moon-ruled sign could fill an ocean with the tears you shed on a daily
basis over everything, from a slight inconvenience to a decades-old playground
brawl you haven't gotten over yet. We'd ask you to forgive us for what we say in this
chapter, but forgiving isn't really your thing. Neither is forgetting. In fact, you crabs
love nothing more than to stay holed up in your shell, counting grudges like precious
jewels. At least that means you won't be out ruining another birthday party with
your legendary ability to bring down the mood.

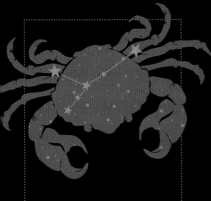

5 NOTORIOUS CANCERS

DATES
June 21–July 22

SYMBOL
Crab

RULER PLANET
The Moon

ELEMENT
Water

MODALITY
Cardinal

OPPOSING SIGN
Capricorn

MORTAL ENEMY
Sagittarius

PET PEEVES
Insufficient gratitude, egotistical people, forgotten birthdays, endings

Sure, Cancers may be able to boast about counting beloved figures such as Meryl Streep, Nelson Mandela, and Princess Diana among their big-hearted ranks, but what if we told you these people were the exception, and not the rule? Moody and vengeful, these hypersensitive signs are far better represented by the following infamous individuals:

1 **Henry VIII (June 28, 1491):** Infamous monarch who started the Church of England just so he could get a divorce. He would go on to have six wives, two of whom he beheaded.

2 **Mike Tyson (June 30, 1966):** American boxing champ and felon best known for biting off one of his opponent's ears during a match.

3 **Lizzie Borden (July 19, 1860):** American ax murderer who was accused of killing her father and stepmother with "forty whacks" from an ax in their family home.

4 **Julius Caesar (July 12/13, 100 BC):** Roman ruler whose dictatorial style led to his assassination by members of his own senate on March 15, 44 BC.

5 **John Dillinger (June 22, 1903):** American Depression-era gangster who robbed 24 banks and four police stations as leader of the Dillinger gang. He was imprisoned multiple times and escaped twice.

Cancer in a nutshell

Most astrologers will tell you that your big emotions are your strength, but that's not the whole truth. Your moody, secretive, grudge-holding sign will waste its life away mulling over pointless worries, perceived slights, and worst-case scenarios. It's no wonder that you're represented by the crab, because your constant bad mood can often cause you to snap, leaving a serious bruise on anyone who dares get in your way.

Your sign loves to wallow in the negative and has not yet found a doorstep it can't darken with its constant catastrophizing. Even worse, your moon-ruled sign changes moods like the tides, so loved ones never know which version of you they're going to get: the weepy, overly needy clinger or the aloof, standoffish wallflower. Either way, they know every conversation is going to revolve around you and your myriad problems, real or imagined. Though, let's be honest, we all know it's the imagined ones that really get you going.

MOODY

Gloomy Cancers live their life enslaved by their ever-changing moods, which usually range from "lightly downtrodden" to "exceedingly devastated." This is where your crab-like nature can really get the best of friends, coworkers, family, and anyone else within snapping distance. It is impossible for others to know what might trigger one of your notorious moods, probably because you hardly know for yourself. As one of the most pessimistic signs in the Zodiac, you have a way of infecting any situation—even a child's birthday party—with your "What's the point?" outlook. With Cancers, the glass isn't just "half empty," it's "half empty and about to explode."

MANIPULATIVE

Cancers are known for being in tune with their own emotions, which makes them experts at manipulating those of others. Crabs will do anything to get their emotional needs met, even if they have to tell a few lies or keep a few secrets to make it happen. These signs project so much emotional neediness it can blind those around them to how cold and calculating they truly are. Masters of the passive-aggressive note, sullen sigh, and backhanded compliment, moon-ruled Cancers have a way of manipulating the emotions of everyone around them with its invisible pull. In the end, they'll have gotten everything they wanted and everyone else will be left feeling drained and bamboozled. No wonder this sign hates spending time in the Sun. They're emotional vampires.

VINDICTIVE

Quick, Cancer! List every person who has ever wronged you. We know you can. Vengeful, vindictive Cancers love nothing more than to snap their claws onto a grudge and hold on for dear life. This overly sensitive sign takes everything personally and will never forget when someone crosses one of their many invisible lines. Given their ever-expanding list of enemies, a happy Cancer is one who gets to exist in a constant state of *schadenfreude*—the German word for "pleasure derived from someone else's misfortune." Uh-oh! Facebook says Cathy just lost her dream job? Well, maybe she should have thought about that before pegging you with a dodgeball in seventh grade...

Cancer placements

Even when you don't have Cancer as your sun sign, these manipulative crabs have a way of getting their claws in any chart where they appear. Bad vibes are kind of infectious that way.

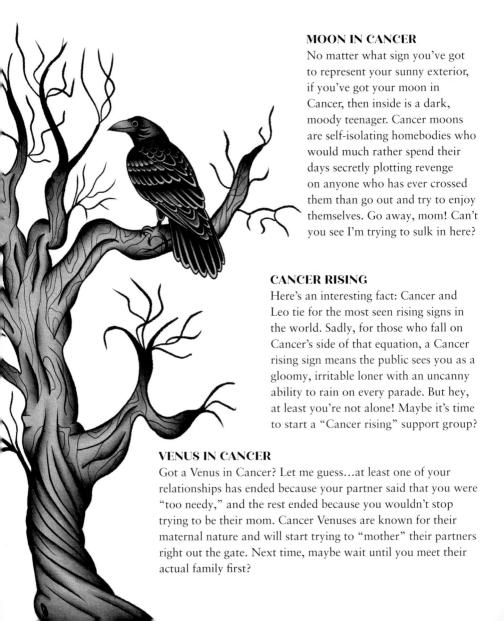

MOON IN CANCER

No matter what sign you've got to represent your sunny exterior, if you've got your moon in Cancer, then inside is a dark, moody teenager. Cancer moons are self-isolating homebodies who would much rather spend their days secretly plotting revenge on anyone who has ever crossed them than go out and try to enjoy themselves. Go away, mom! Can't you see I'm trying to sulk in here?

CANCER RISING

Here's an interesting fact: Cancer and Leo tie for the most seen rising signs in the world. Sadly, for those who fall on Cancer's side of that equation, a Cancer rising sign means the public sees you as a gloomy, irritable loner with an uncanny ability to rain on every parade. But hey, at least you're not alone! Maybe it's time to start a "Cancer rising" support group?

VENUS IN CANCER

Got a Venus in Cancer? Let me guess...at least one of your relationships has ended because your partner said that you were "too needy," and the rest ended because you wouldn't stop trying to be their mom. Cancer Venuses are known for their maternal nature and will start trying to "mother" their partners right out the gate. Next time, maybe wait until you meet their actual family first?

Cancer in love

Mariah Carey's hit "Obsessed" may have been about a Libra (the rapper Eminem), but it should have been about you, Cancer. Obsessively loyal, Cancers will hold onto a relationship long past its expiration date simply because things like "letting go" and "moving on" are not in their repertoire. Once a crab lets someone inside their shell, there is no going back. On the off chance someone is able to extricate themselves from Cancer's grip and become their ex, they'll have made an enemy for life. Cancer does not take emotional betrayal lightly. They're still not over the time their middle school infatuation danced with somebody else.

SINGLE CANCER

Single Cancers love to play hard to get, but it really is just that—a game. They'll ignore a person's texts while simultaneously lurking on their social media and following their every move. And if they just happen to show up at the very same coffee shop their crush just posted about going to every day? Well, isn't that just one more sign from the universe that they're meant to be together? Cancers are the sign most often to find themselves locked in a "situationship" because of their penchant for pursuing the unavailable. They'll waste years pining away over an unrequited love rather than moving on to pursue someone attainable. Then what would they have to complain about?

CANCER IN A RELATIONSHIP

We don't know about crabs, but Cancers mate for life. Once they're in a relationship (either real or imagined), Cancers are almost impossible to break up with. Try, and you'll be met with a moody, passive-aggressive guilt-tripper who won't allow the relationship to end until they get "closure," usually in the form of multiple hours-long conversations that leave the other party too emotionally drained to follow through with the split. As a partner, Cancer is jealous and secretive. They'll go silent at dinner and leave it up to their beau to figure out why. (Hint: It probably has something to do with the "flirty" server who refilled your breadsticks.)

Most compatible

Cancer + Capricorn

Are you a Cancer looking to make things work for the long haul? Then you're gonna want to find yourself a Capricorn. These tetchy signs will bond over their shared negative outlook and love of staying home. Cancer will never have to worry about Capricorn's ability to commit (it's what they do), and Capricorn will have no problem putting in the work required to get Cancer to open up. Once these two homebodies pair up, they'll never leave each other—or the couch.

Least compatible

Cancer + Sagittarius

Water and fire? Yeah… that's gonna cause some problems. Sagittarius's unserious nature and penchant for ribbing loved ones will get under Cancer's hypersensitive skin in an instant. Even worse, Sagittarius's inability to stay in one place or make a commitment will drive Cancer crazy as they try in vain to get their archer partner to settle down. Let this relationship go too far, and Cancer might spend their whole life pining after this sign even though they know it won't work—maybe even because they know it won't work out.

Cancer + Aries

Another fire sign, Aries likes to get hot and heavy fast, whereas Cancer prefers to take things slow and allow emotional bonds to develop over time. This slow-moving pace will infuriate Aries, who will in turn overwhelm Cancer with big shows of affection right out the gate. If they're able to get over the initial mismatch, trouble will still arise from Aries' wandering eye, which will fuel Cancer's jealousy and cause them to lash out. Once they do, Aries will be more than happy to let the argument explode rather than talk things through rationally. Avoid this pairing unless you want yet another ex you refuse to be in the same room with.

Cancer + Gemini

When needy Cancer gets together with commitment-phobic Gemini, there are bound to be some tears—on Cancer's end, that is. Gemini has what it takes to charm their way through Cancer's hard shell, but by the time they do they'll probably have moved on to their next romantic pursuit, leaving Cancer feeling exposed and betrayed. Empathic Cancer will be driven mad by Gemini's ever-changing emotions, and Gemini will be bored to tears by Cancer's need to constantly discuss heavy, emotional topics. Let's just say these two are better off as friends. If they can even manage that…

CANCER AT WORK

You know that coworker who silently fumes in the corner of the meeting and never says a word, but sends an extremely detailed, passive-aggressive email later that day about everything that was wrong? That's you, Cancer. The Zodiac's constant buzzkill, coworkers know not to come to you with a new idea or project unless they want to hear all the ways it could go awry. Depressing and unproductive to be around, you've probably noticed the way people avoid your desk like the plague, lest they be drawn into one of your lengthy mope sessions about the boss who never listens or the coworker who wronged you. Speaking of coworkers who wronged you, you keep a detailed list of them in your desk and spend at least half the workday fantasizing about when you will exact your revenge. You love nothing more than to feel superior at work, and will often take jobs you're overqualified for just to complain about how overqualified you are. The same goes for working late, which you'll volunteer to do mostly for the sulking rights they afford you later. When annual review time comes around, your boss knows to be prepared for a meltdown, as you take even the most constructive criticism very, very personally. Honestly, someone should probably check your desk for voodoo dolls the next time you're out of the office.

CANCER IN THE FAMILY

Mom? Is that you? Maternal Cancer loves to take on the role of matriarch, whether or not they actually are one. You are obsessed with family in a way that starts off as endearing but ends up creepy to anyone who bears witness to hours-long phone calls home. Relatives know to expect an incoming of texts about how much you "miss" them any time they don't make family their top priority. You love nothing more than to take on the role of the long-suffering sibling who stayed home to take care of mom and dad, just so you can guilt-trip anyone who dared move away. This fierce loyalty to family often means you're the in-law from hell for anyone who dares enter the clan, and you're not above delivering a slightly too-long weepy wedding speech about how the bride or groom to be is "taking your baby away."

CANCER AT HOME

There's a reason Cancer is represented by an animal that carries its home on its back. For your sign, home is everything. No wonder it's so difficult to get you to leave. Cancer's home is the place where you feel most comfortable to be yourself, which is why it's always a little bit depressing. Windows closed, shades drawn, and a pile of blankets to show where you last wallowed in your own despair, the Cancer residence is a sanctuary for your own moodiness. When the rare guest is allowed inside the den, the dreary-yet-elaborate surroundings will leave them feeling more like they just stepped into a haunted mansion than a person's living room. On the bright side, your obsession with domesticity means you are clean and meticulous when it comes to keeping house. Unfortunately, your solitary sign keeps *chez* Cancer locked up tighter than a bank vault, so there's rarely anyone around to admire your handiwork.

CANCER AND TRAVEL

Leaving the house? Cancer? We'll believe it when we see it. Cancers hate to be without their creature comforts, so the hurdle required to actually get them to go anywhere can often be insurmountable. When you do decide to take a trip, you bring your doom-and-gloom attitude along for the ride and cannot help but draw attention to everything that might go wrong. What if your luggage gets lost? What if you get lost? What if your hotel is hit by an asteroid? It's all on the table for your pessimistic star sign. Even the most minor travel delay or language barrier will send you into a homesick spiral. Cancers have a knack of finding the worst in everything, especially accommodation, which will never match up to the haven they've built at home. And you're not happy to just privately pout, either. You must bring everyone down with your constant complaining. With Cancer, every vacation is turned into a guilt-trip, since you love nothing more than to "compromise" with the group, only to hold it over their heads later. You'll spend an entire dinner silently seething that you didn't get your choice of restaurant and taking passive-aggressive jabs at your table mates. In short, everyone would be better off if you just stayed home and watched the Travel Channel.

The two sides of Cancer

Watery, emotional Cancer is considered one of the Zodiac's "feminine" signs, but their temperamental nature means they can swing into their masculine at any moment, regardless of gender identity. Those on the receiving end of one of your mood swings might feel like they're dealing with two completely different people, but underneath it all is just the same gloomy crab out to ruin everyone's day with their bad vibes.

CANCER DARK MASCULINE

Moody and aloof, a Cancer who is engaging in their dark masculine side may think they appear strong and stoic, when they're actually just being a curmudgeon. Getting this version of Cancer out of the house is an even more Herculean task than usual, as they are typically feeling solitary and antisocial. Probably for the best. No one needs that kind of a cloud over their night out anyway.

CANCER DARK FEMININE

Naturally femme Cancer will often find themselves engaging in their dark feminine side, which is just as moody and gloomy as their dark masculine but with an extra dose of neediness and passive aggression. The ultimate martyr, a Cancer situated in their dark feminine loves to "sacrifice" for their loved ones, but only so that they can play the role of the long-suffering mother for weeks after. Poor, unfortunate crab. You have it so hard.

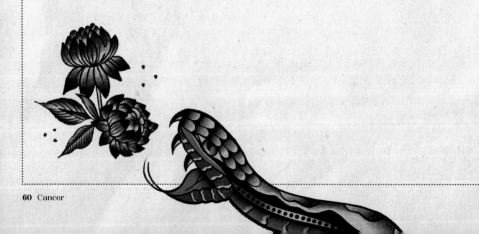

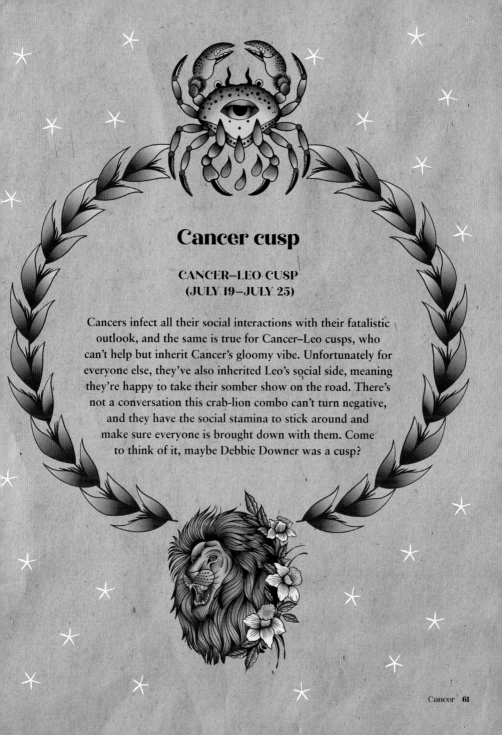

Cancer cusp

CANCER–LEO CUSP
(JULY 19–JULY 25)

Cancers infect all their social interactions with their fatalistic outlook, and the same is true for Cancer–Leo cusps, who can't help but inherit Cancer's gloomy vibe. Unfortunately for everyone else, they've also inherited Leo's social side, meaning they're happy to take their somber show on the road. There's not a conversation this crab-lion combo can't turn negative, and they have the social stamina to stick around and make sure everyone is brought down with them. Come to think of it, maybe Debbie Downer was a cusp?

Hello Leo

You're so vain, you probably think this chapter is about you. And for once, you're actually right. Not that you'd ever admit it if you weren't. You're represented by the lion, aka the king of the jungle. Fitting really, since you tend to think your word is law. There isn't a mirror in the world you can't get lost staring into—and you haven't found a flaw yet. Probably for the best, since your image-obsessed sign is all about how you look on the outside. Unfortunately, that leaves little room for self-improvement or introspection. In the end, your obsession with appearances leaves you blind to what people really see when they look your way: a gaudy, self-obsessed know-it-all who'd rather chase fame and fortune than work toward something real.

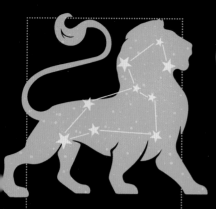

DATES
July 23–August 22

SYMBOL
Lion

RULER PLANET
The Sun

ELEMENT
Fire

MODALITY
Fixed

OPPOSING SIGN
Aquarius

MORTAL ENEMY
Taurus

PET PEEVES
Being ignored, public callouts, back talk, bad dressers

5 NOTORIOUS LEOS

Fame-loving Leo can boast many A-list names among its ranks, from Jennifer Lopez to Mick Jagger to Whitney Houston, but it's the dark side of Leo that truly represents what this sign has to offer. Here are five notorious Leos who have changed history, sometimes for the worse:

1 **Elizabeth Bathory (August 7, 1560):** Hungarian countess known as "Countess Dracula" due to her love of human blood. According to legend, she used to bathe in blood, believing it would keep her young.

2 **Mata Hari (August 7, 1876):** Dutch exotic dancer and courtesan who was convicted of using her feminine wiles to spy for Germany in World War I and executed by firing squad.

3 **Napoleon Bonaparte (August 15, 1769):** French Emperor and general who conquered much of Europe during his reign. He was forced to abdicate the throne twice and lived his final days in exile on a remote island.

4 **Alfred Hitchcock (August 13, 1899):** American filmmaker who directed some of the most iconic horror movies. His obsession with "icy blondes" like Grace Kelly and Kim Novak is visible throughout his movies.

5 **Coco Chanel (August 19, 1883):** French fashion designer whose signature style gave us the Chanel suit. After the liberation of Paris in 1944, she was accused of serving as an informant for the Nazis when her affair with a German officer became public.

Leo in a nutshell

We're not even going to bother going over how nice astrologers typically say you are, Leo. You praise yourself enough as it is. Instead, we're going to get right to the heart of the matter. Leos are narcissistic, entitled megalomaniacs who see nothing beyond their own myopic worldview. Your preening sign is as shallow as they come, and has the garish fashion sense to prove it. You build your entire life around your "look at me!" mentality. And—good news—people are looking. Though they don't necessarily like what they see. At a party, you're the person who sucks up all the oxygen by prattling on about everything on your mind, blithely unaware that your friends may also have something to contribute to the conversation. And by friends, we really mean followers. King Leos would much rather surround themselves with sycophants than risk allowing someone into their inner circle who might actually tell them like it is. Unfortunately for you, that's our job. Let's get started, shall we?

VAIN

Quick, Leo! When was the last time you looked in the mirror? Just kidding. You're probably looking in one right now. Your image-obsessed sign can't help but spend every waking moment crafting what they consider the perfect exterior. A quick trip down Leo's social media page will likely reveal an endless scroll of perfectly posed pictures and filtered selfies. Not pictured? Friends, family, or a single hobby other than smiling for the camera. Leos may think of themselves as irreproachable objects of envy with a mighty roar, but one simple question will leave them totally undone—did you know there's something in your teeth?

SELF-OBSESSED

When your ruling planet is the Sun, it's hardly a surprise that you think the world revolves around you. Leos are typically concerned with just three things: me, me, and me. Other people's thoughts and feelings are simply not their concern. In fact, they probably don't even register as you mindlessly move along on your never-ending quest for world domination. And who better to rule the world than you, the best, smartest, and most beautiful person ever to walk the Earth? Unfortunately, even if you do succeed on your mad quest, you'll have no one to share your spoils with, thanks to all the feelings you've hurt along the way. For your sign, it truly is lonely at the top.

CONDESCENDING

Leos know best. At least, they think they do. And they're willing to say so—loudly and often. Pompous and overbearing, you can hardly conceive of a world in which someone else's opinion would be worth considering. Your puffed-up sign has no problem deriding anyone whose thoughts differ from your own, even if the facts are on their side. In fact, the more you're proven wrong, the more likely you are to dig in, employing childish insults, adolescent eye rolls, and toddler-inspired tantrums to bully naysayers into agreement. At least the mean girls of the world are impressed.

Leo placements

In the same way that Leo takes over any room it enters, so it takes over any birth chart in which it appears. Got Leo as one of your "big three"? Well, then you may as well have it at the top of your chart because this sun-ruled sign has a way of outshining all of the others.

MOON IN LEO

Leo moons are spotlight chasers, obsessively fixated on making sure all eyes are on them. They spend every waking moment strategizing new ways to get attention, and aren't above petty tricks like bursting into tears or "losing" an earring to make it happen.

LEO RISING

If being seen is your goal—and let's be honest, it is—then congratulations! You are seen. As a conceited, tacky, blow-hard with little to offer outside your impeccable photo-editing skills. You always said you wanted to get people talking. You just didn't realize that it would be behind your back.

VENUS IN LEO

Got your Venus in Leo? Then be prepared to spend your whole life searching for a partner who is as obsessed with you as you are. Venus Leos are great at initially attracting partners with their shiny magnetism, but often repel them later with their high-maintenance tendencies and inability to retain information about anyone other than themselves. It's one thing to ask someone if they have any siblings on a first date, but after a year of dating it's kind of another story...

Leo in love

Leos enjoy living their lives in love with exactly one person: themselves. Everyone else, even their partner, comes second. When it comes to searching for a life partner, Leos need someone who is exactly as in love with themselves as they are and willing to go along with whatever they say without question. They need a partner who is happy to shower them with a constant stream of praise and leave no doubt as to the level of their devotion. Leos would date themselves if they could, but a fawning doormat will do just as well.

SINGLE LEO

Single Leo is all about quantity over quality. You'd much rather surround yourself with a gaggle of adoring potential suitors than put in the work it takes to find an equal partner. Plus, an endless parade of first dates lets you indulge in two of your favorite activities: getting dressed up and talking about yourself. Hours can go by before you notice you haven't asked your date a single question, and you hardly care if they're enjoying themselves...so long as they pick up the check. Once you part ways, it's out of sight, out of mind. Probably why you're one of the rare people who has never been ghosted. You'd have to save their number for that.

LEO IN A RELATIONSHIP

Once Leo finds someone who is sufficiently enamored with them, their romance tends to burn hot and heavy. Leos are high-maintenance lovers who expect nothing less than complete loyalty from their partner, who they regard more as an accessory than a full human. This is probably why you tend to go for people who can add to your own status and allure (or are just plain rich). You want someone powerful and influential, with the important caveat that they never become more powerful or influential than yourself. The moment they do, you'll kick them to the curb—usually without doing them the courtesy of informing them that it's over.

Most compatible

Leo + Libra

Leo's ultimate match is a Libra. Air fuels fire when this match gets together, and Leo will love the way beauty-obsessed Libra gasses them up with praise for their physical appearance. These front-facing signs love all the same things: style, socializing, and being seen. Plus, Libra's indecisive nature means they'll have no problem letting Leo make all the decisions. Just how Leo likes it.

Least compatible

Leo + Capricorn

The mismatch between social butterfly and homebody will stop this pairing dead in its tracks. Flashy Leo and low-key Capricorn have almost nothing in common and will find themselves constantly at odds on how to spend their time together. While Capricorn would love nothing more than to stay at home and watch their favorite comfort show, Leo sees no point in getting into a relationship if they can't show it off to the masses. Capricorn will chafe at Leo's need for outside approval, while Leo will find themselves constantly cringing at Capricorn's lack of social graces. The moment Capricorn embarrasses Leo at a party by not knowing who everyone's latest reality TV obsession is, they'll be out the door for good.

Leo + Cancer

Leo can't stand anyone who wants to rain on their parade, and gloomy Cancer will do just that. These two will butt heads constantly over their opposing worldviews, and overly cheery Leo will always come off as fake to pessimistic Cancer. Leo's navel-gazing will mean they'll never put in the work needed to get through Cancer's tough exterior, and their inability to consider other people's feelings will send hypersensitive Cancer into an emotional tailspin. Ultimately, all the ugly crying and emotional vulnerability will give Leo the ick faster than Cancer can say, "What are we?"

Leo + Aries

Aries' hot-and-heavy and obsessive approach to love will certainly get Leo's attention at first, but once the novelty wears off and Aries' eye starts to wander, it'll be constant clashes for these two. This fire-on-fire pair will lead to explosive fights as neither will ever want to compromise. Plus, competitive Aries will always try to one-up Leo, something lions absolutely cannot tolerate in a partner. Leo may allow themselves to get caught up in a vicious makeup-and-breakup cycle with Aries, but only for the attention that the constant emotional turmoil will then bring.

LEO AT WORK

In the workplace Leo bravado mixes with an acute case of imposter syndrome to create a toxic situation for everyone involved. On the one hand, you believe you should be the boss, regardless of where you actually stand in the chain of command. On the other hand, you're desperate to hide even the smallest insecurities from your coworkers, and act out of a constant fear they'll discover you have no idea what you're doing. The mix of insecurity and ego means you go overboard projecting an air of confidence, even when the whole team would be better served if you just sat back and listened. Leo is that coworker who makes a big show of how busy they are, but when push comes to shove people will be hard pressed to figure out what exactly it is that you do all day. The answer? Scrolling social media and keeping jealous tabs on all the people you can't help but compare yourself to. It's a tough job, but somebody's gotta do it!

LEO IN THE FAMILY

For spotlight-loving Leo every day is the Leo show. And boy, do your family members know it. As far as you're concerned, every family member is the spare to your heir, and you tend to see them more as loyal servants than equals. And sure, Leos are known for being extremely generous with family and loved ones...if they agree to get on their knees and kiss the ring. Your showboating sign hates to share anything, even DNA. This can lead to a competitive streak with siblings, cousins, and even your own grandma if she's getting too much attention. Who said her 90th birthday party should be about her, anyway? Like most monarchs, you keep a jealous eye on all of your next of kin, just in case one of them gets any ideas about stealing the throne. At the first whiff of dissent, you'll have your ill-fated family member locked up in the tower faster than they can muster troops for a rebellion. Ruthless to a fault, you have no problem putting their head on a spike in front of the family vacation home to send a message to any other young upstarts (aka your nieces and nephews) who may consider coming for your crown. Long live the king!

LEO AND TRAVEL

Leo's preferred method of travel is probably palanquin, but barring that, first class will do. Your "go big or go home" ethos goes triple for travel, and you see no point in booking a vacation to anywhere other than the lap of luxury. From hotel rooms to restaurants, Leos need everything to be five-star. Any attempt to shrink expenses by their travel companions will be met by Leo's signature scorn. Speaking of travel companions, they'd better be okay with being conscripted into Leo's personal photography team. You take "pics or it didn't happen" to a whole new level when you travel, and need to make sure every outfit—which you bought specifically for the trip and planned weeks in advance—is meticulously documented. For Leos, travel is less about enjoying the vacation than it is about making sure

other people can see that they're enjoying their vacation. That's why half of your friends secretly mute you any time they know you're about to go away, lest their feeds are flooded with an endless stream of perfectly posed photos alerting them to your every move. And if your Trevi Fountain sunset pics come out less than stellar, there's always Photoshop. Your fans—I mean friends—expect perfection.

LEO AT HOME

Gold toilets, velvet tapestries, and richly upholstered chaises—is this the Playboy Mansion, or *chez* Leo? Leo sees their home as their own personal Versailles, and decorates accordingly. Most people would feel a little odd putting their own portrait up on the wall, but you're not most people, are you, Leo? You subscribe to a strict "bigger is better" policy, especially when it comes to your home. You won't be truly happy until you're pacing your palatial floor plan, watching a massive flatscreen from your equally enormous sectional, and sleeping the

night away on a mattress that could fit a small family. You'd probably describe your taste as "high-end" to whichever unfortunate interior decorator you employ to execute your vision, but they'll soon find that "gaudy" is a lot more like it. The concepts "stealth wealth" and "quiet luxury" are foreign to your sign, which puts the ability to show off above all other concerns. Unfortunately for you, fame chaser, this is exactly why the true elites will always steer clear of your gold-encrusted path.

The two sides of Leo

As a fire sign, Leo tends to fall on the masculine side of the Zodiac. But within every Leo lies a dark masculine and dark feminine side, lurking and waiting to be unleashed. Not sure which side of the king-size bed you woke up on today? Here's how you can tell Leo's dark masculine from its dark feminine.

LEO DARK MASCULINE

Talk about a Napoleon complex—a Leo that's situated in its dark masculine is confident to the point of megalomania. They see the whole world as one big kingdom to be conquered, and they have no problem stepping on lesser mortals to get to the top. Move over Louis XIV, the real Sun King has arrived.

LEO DARK FEMININE

When a Leo is expressing their dark feminine side the whole world has to stop and stare. They'll stop at nothing to get all eyes on them, even if their loud, garish behavior earns them more than a few dirty looks. So what? As long as it's your name that's on people's lips, dark feminine Leo is happy. Just be sure you don't hear what anyone is actually saying.

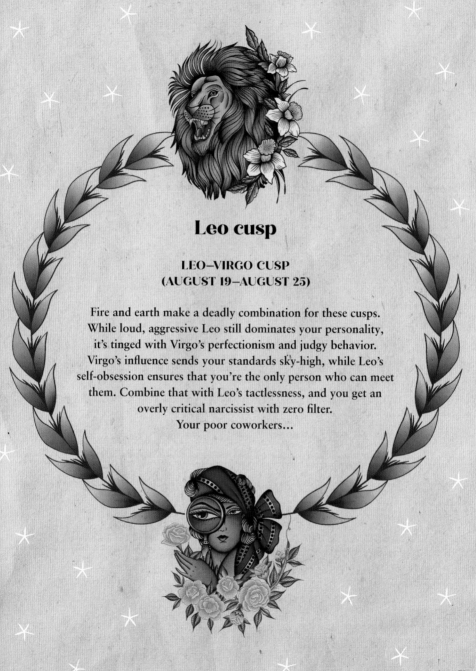

Leo cusp

LEO–VIRGO CUSP
(AUGUST 19–AUGUST 25)

Fire and earth make a deadly combination for these cusps.
While loud, aggressive Leo still dominates your personality,
it's tinged with Virgo's perfectionism and judgy behavior.
Virgo's influence sends your standards sky-high, while Leo's
self-obsession ensures that you're the only person who can meet
them. Combine that with Leo's tactlessness, and you get an
overly critical narcissist with zero filter.
Your poor coworkers…

Hello Virgo...

You may think nobody can be harder on you than you are on yourself, Virgo, but we're not worried. You may love nothing more than to impose your rigid standards on everyone around you, but the fact of the matter is you're far from perfect yourself. Not only are you famous for letting perfect be the enemy of the good, you take it one step further and turn "perfect" into a dam that stops all progress. Your pathological need to go over minute details ad nauseam makes you a menace to everything from morning meetings to friendly game nights. You just can't help yourself. You have to ensure that every rule of Monopoly is followed to the letter, even if that gets in the way of fun. Luckily, "fun" is not something you'd ever be accused of being.

DATES
August 23–
September 22

SYMBOL
Virgin

RULER PLANET
Mercury

ELEMENT
Earth

MODALITY
Mutable

OPPOSING SIGN
Pisces

MORTAL ENEMY
Sagittarius

PET PEEVES
Missed deadlines, typos,
tardiness, mess

5 NOTORIOUS VIRGOS

Let's get this out of the way right now: yes, Beyoncé is a Virgo. But when this perfection-chasing sign goes wrong, it goes way, way wrong. Here are five famous Virgos who used their sign's analytical powers for less than noble means:

1 **Ivan the Terrible (August 25, 1530):** The first tsar of Russia who callously executed thousands of people during his reign and even killed his own son for trying to go against his will.

2 **Louis XVI (August 23, 1754):** French monarch and husband of Marie Antoinette who failed to endear himself to the French people. His unfortunate reign ended with the French Revolution and the removal of his head via guillotine.

3 **Caligula (August 31, 12 AD):** Roman emperor known for his cruel and unusual behavior. During his short reign he was accused of torturing senate members who disagreed with him.

4 **Elizabeth I (September 7, 1533):** The "Virgin Queen" of England who famously reigned without marrying in order to hold onto power. She eventually named James I as her heir, but not before beheading his mother—Mary, Queen of Scots—for treason.

5 **Whitey Bulger (September 3, 1929):** American crime boss who was sentenced to two life sentences. Despite being #2 on the FBI's Ten Most Wanted Fugitives list in 1999, he evaded capture for over a decade until an anonymous tip led to his arrest in 2011.

Virgo in a nutshell

How does it feel to be the Zodiac's consummate buzzkill? By now you've probably gotten used to the wave of side-eyes that greet you anytime you walk into a room. The moment Virgo enters, everyone knows the party is officially over.

It's not often that someone is as outwardly critical and inwardly self-hating as you. You should honestly give yourself some credit for being as mean to yourself as you are to others—not that you'd ever outwardly praise yourself for anything. You'd much rather toil in private, tinkering away at your masterpiece but never revealing it to the public for fear that it's "not good enough." Unfortunately for those around you, you don't limit these harsh critiques to yourself. Your penchant for meanness under the guise of "truth telling" means your friends learned to stop asking your opinion long ago, but that's no matter. You're a master of unsolicited advice, and will share your critiques whether they're asked for or not. This is probably why your social circle is so small. Those who can't take the heat got out of the kitchen a long time ago.

PERFECTIONIST

"What's wrong with perfection?" You say this to yourself, as you pore over the 50th draft of a company-wide email about the proper way to label a file. As one of the Zodiac's fixed signs, you hate change, and you use your perfectionism as a cudgel to make sure it never happens. Nothing is ever good enough for you, which means you spend your days constantly revising old work rather than moving on to something new. Your analytical eye makes you an excellent editor (or tax collector), as you love nothing more than to obsess over a lengthy document of errors. Actually, there is something you love more—telling the author about all of the errors you found...in the harshest terms possible.

PEDANTIC

When your perfectionism isn't enough to grind the gears of progress to a halt, your pedanticism will. Those who know you realize that getting trapped in a conversation with you will mean an endless cycle of minor corrections that will be enough to bring any real conversation to a halt. You just don't know how to let a misused word or an inelegantly phrased sentence go, even if the speaker's meaning was clear to everyone else. You see every conversation as an opportunity to show off your impressive intellect and make others feel small in the process. By the time you're done picking apart their story, your coworker will rue the day they decided to tell you about their weekend. Serves them right for saying "literally" when they actually meant "figuratively." Rude.

PESSIMISTIC

When critiquing a project to death isn't enough to stop it moving forward, you pull out the final tool in your arsenal: a detailed list of everything that could go wrong. Sure, your impressive powers of analysis might be used for something like solving world hunger, but why do that when you could instead use it to ideate incessantly on all the ways solving world hunger would contribute to the Earth's overpopulation issue? You're a master at finding the downside to everything, from trying a new restaurant to your friend's decision to adopt a dog. You just can't hold back telling them about the time your aunt adopted a dog only to discover it had an incontinence problem that could only be solved with expensive surgery. What's that? You're just trying to help prepare them for the inevitable...

Virgo placements

Virgo tends to be a more subtle sign, but if it appears in one of your birth chart's "big three" there's no way you're not going to feel the effects. Virgo does its work under the surface, meaning it will get under your skin eventually.

MOON IN VIRGO

If you're born with your moon in Virgo, it means that your inner monologue is a constant stream of critiques. You may look like you're engaged in conversation, but you're really clocking every single thing that could be improved about your surroundings (those fire escapes aren't up to code), your companions (Theresa's new haircut is a little crooked), and, most importantly, yourself (Why did I just say that? Do these people even like me? I bet they don't like me...). Honestly, we're depressed for you.

VENUS IN VIRGO

People with their Venus in Virgo like to say they're "realists" when it comes to love. We'd like to say they're cynical defeatists obsessed with looking for reasons it can't work. Virgo Venuses hate all the things most people find romantic, like passion, affection, and spontaneous gestures. Instead, they prefer a person who can methodically check boxes off on the "perfect partner" spreadsheet they've been maintaining since they were ten years old. At least nobody can ever accuse them of not knowing what they want.

VIRGO RISING

When your rising sign is in Virgo it means the world sees you as an anal-retentive control freak in desperate need of a chill pill. Sure, they may also know they can rely on you for anything work- or organization-related, but that doesn't typically translate to being included in many social events later on. Maybe you should become a party planner? Then they'll have to invite you.

Virgo in love

A Virgo's love language is simple: critique. Your perfection-obsessed sign expects nothing less than the very best from everyone, and your unfortunate romantic partners are no exception. Those who enter into a relationship with you can expect a partnership that's low on physical affection, but high on nitpicking and castigation. It's not that you don't *like* physical affection—you just like it performed in a highly methodical way. (And you will require a shower both before and after.) As a Virgo you prefer to whip your partner into shape and, as an added bonus, they get a front-row seat to your constant negativity and pessimistic obsessing. No wonder so many of them end up as sad as you.

SINGLE VIRGO

In many ways, a single Virgo is a happy Virgo. (If there even is such a thing as a happy Virgo.) You'd rather be alone forever than have to put up with someone who can't meet your sky-high standards. And you've yet to find anyone that can.

Being single also reinforces Virgo's negative self-image, which already says you deserve to be alone until you've finally achieved true perfection. In this case, misery does not love company.

VIRGO IN A RELATIONSHIP

In a relationship with a Virgo? Then you may be entitled to financial compensation. Virgos love to turn their critical eye toward those closest to them, and who is closer than the person who shares your bed? (Which, by the way, you forgot to make properly.) The closer Virgo and their partner get, the more constant the stream of admonishment becomes. Virgos say they prize "truth" above all else in a relationship, but it just so happens that the "truth," as they see it, never involves them being in the wrong. In the end, they'd rather cut and run than budge when differences arise. The relationship was just a distraction from their quest for perfection anyway.

Most compatible

Virgo + Pisces

Fantasy meets reality when these two pair up, and the results are actually a loving, stable relationship. Dreamy Pisces' rose-colored glasses mean they see Virgo's constant stream of criticism for what it is: an expression of love. So long as Virgo provides a stable foundation (which they will), Pisces' legendary insecurity won't be triggered, leaving only their best qualities to come into play—compassion, empathy, and optimism. They can help Virgo break out of their glass-half-empty shell, while Virgo will provide Pisces with the structure they need to follow through on some of those big ideas. Anyone who thinks a dreamer and a realist can't make it work simply hasn't seen these two in action.

Least compatible

Virgo + Gemini

Geminis are simply far too messy and unpredictable for you, Virgo. You may initially be attracted to them, thinking they're a "fixer-upper" you can mold to your standards, but you'll quickly find that Gemini is a sign that cannot be tamed. Geminis have no problem challenging every aspect of your worldview, without realizing that arguments they see as simply an intellectual exercise actually cut you to your very core. Not to mention the fact that their tolerance for dirty dishes will have you out the door the moment you first step foot in their apartment.

Virgo + Sagittarius

Someone who is meaner to you than you are? No thanks. When Virgos and Sags get together, both sides are in for a nasty tongue lashing (and we don't mean in the bedroom). Both of these signs pride themselves on "truth telling" via cutting remarks, meaning they are bound to end up in a clash of below-the-belt insults. They may start out thinking that they're just matching wits, but they'll end up hurting each other's feelings. Steer clear of this partnership. You're hard enough on yourself as it is.

Virgo + Aquarius

Aquarius and Virgo fail to connect because they see the world from totally different perspectives. On the one hand, Aquarius is an optimistic big thinker who always has their eye on a distant, idealistic future. On the other, Virgos are pessimists who are consumed with the imperfections of the here and now. These mismatching worldviews mean they'll each drive the other crazy. Virgo will be totally unable to hear Aquarius's vision for a better world, and Aquarius will never stop daydreaming long enough to help with the things that need to be done in the present—like bringing in the groceries or folding the bed sheets.

VIRGO AT WORK

Work is where Virgo thrives—and is at its most deranged. On the one hand, there's no one who can claim you aren't a hard worker. On the other, you take that "hard work" ethos to the point of delusion. In your mind, no one is as thorough, smart, or logical as you, meaning no one else's opinion matters. Even your boss is just an obstacle on the way to true perfection, and you have no problem disregarding their wishes if they contradict your own. Coworkers know to add an extra hour onto any meeting with you, as you cannot help but pepper them with an endless stream of questions and clarifications. They also know better than to come to you for advice or help on a project, since your legendary red pen will surely leave them feeling more demoralized than inspired. You may love critique, but "constructive criticism" is simply not in your wheelhouse. Plus, your obsession with following rules makes your peers want to spend as little time with you as possible, lest you catch wind of any violations. They may come to you when it's time to reorganize the break room, but there will be an office-wide eye roll the next day when they open up their email to a tome from you on proper supply usage and lunch storage protocol.

VIRGO IN THE FAMILY

The perfect family member does not exist, but Virgo will certainly try. The ultimate parents' pet, Virgo will stop at nothing to be the most accomplished, helpful, and service-oriented member of the family. Sure, this makes you the apple of your mother's eye, but it also turns every family gathering into a low-simmering competition. Unlike Aries, who makes their competitive streak known with loud boasting and overt plays for attention, Virgo loves to play the modest martyr while secretly believing they're better than everyone else. If any cousins or siblings offer to help clear the table alongside you, you'll swiftly make them regret that decision by drowning them in a sea of criticism and nitpicking. As much as you love to portray yourself as a humble, family-centered helper, you really see your family members as pawns you can use to display your own perfection and superiority. The ultimate overachiever, you take a family member's choice to live their life outside your own standards personally, and will do everything in your power to correct them into submission. If someone who shares your DNA can have fun, does that mean you can too? You can't even begin to imagine it.

VIRGO AT HOME

Simple, clean lines. White (or off-white) paint. Some people may call the Virgo décor style "minimalist." We call it boring and sterile. Virgos love to live in an environment where they can see how clean things are, which means they prefer to keep everything blindingly white. From their couch to the walls to their always-starched sheets, Virgos like a home that looks like no living creature has ever stepped foot in it, let alone lived there. They cannot abide clutter, meaning every item has a carefully chosen place and must be returned there the moment it is out of use. Every item in the Virgo kitchen is labeled, even if they live alone. Guests will be met with an immediate onslaught of anxiety, as Virgo will never trust an outsider not to ruin the place with their dirt and carelessness. Even minor spills can bring an entire dinner party to a halt as Virgo leaps into action with their five-part spill-cleaning routine. When it comes to the Virgo home, you are not only crying over spilled milk, you're having a full-blown meltdown.

VIRGO AND TRAVEL

Why hire a travel agent when you can just travel with a Virgo? (Answer: because the travel agent won't tag along and anxiously ensure you follow their itinerary to the letter.) Virgos live in a constant state of preparing for the worst, and when traveling that tendency is amplified to the max. You're that person at the airport who checks and rechecks their ticket every 15 minutes (it's still exactly where you left it) and keeps their passport strapped to their chest at all times. Once Virgos arrive at their accommodation, they cannot unpack until they have checked every nook and cranny for dirt and grime, stripped the mattress to look for bugs, and ensured that the front desk is ready to give them a wake-up call promptly at 6am so that they're not late for the early morning museum tour they booked months in advance. For Virgos, vacationing is about efficiency, not relaxation. This means you typically spend more time meticulously planning every moment of your break than you do enjoying it, and leave disappointed because there will always be something that didn't go exactly as you planned. At least you won't be filling anyone's feeds with sugar-coated travel grams anytime soon. You're too busy writing a sternly worded review for your hotel regarding its underwhelming towel softness for that.

The two sides of Virgo

Virgo naturally falls on the feminine side of the Zodiac, but that doesn't mean that its masculine side won't come out to play every once in a while. And by play, of course, we mean work. This is Virgo, after all. Here are the two sides of the Virgo coin onto which anyone can fall depending on the day.

VIRGO DARK MASCULINE

When a Virgo is situated in its dark masculine, they are all business and low-simmering ambition. They have no problem barking orders at lesser mortals (read: everyone) and wear their pet peeves clearly on their sleeve. Like a cold, distant father who is impossible to please, dark masculine Virgos often exist in a state of stoic silence. They don't really have anything nice to say, and so they don't say anything at all.

VIRGO DARK FEMININE

When a Virgo is in their dark feminine, you'll only find out what they're feeling through a series of passive-aggressive actions and telling gestures, such as rewashing the dishes after you've already done them because the work was not up to par. A dark feminine Virgo spends their days obsessively organizing and reorganizing their living space, only to do every task all over again the moment a new speck of dust appears. Introverted and shy, dark feminine Virgos will never tell a guest outright to take their shoes off in the hall, but they'll get the hint when they hear the faint sounds of scrubbing the moment they walk out the door.

Virgo cusp

VIRGO–LIBRA CUSP
(SEPTEMBER 19–SEPTEMBER 25)

Earthy Virgo loves to hang back and keep a watchful eye on the world, while airy Libra wants nothing more than to stay above the fray. When they combine, you get a chilly, detached observer who loves standing on the sidelines and feeling superior. These cusp-ers have lots of opinions on how things should be done, but they'd never let themselves get emotionally involved enough to share them. Instead, they turn their critical gaze inward and spend their days perfecting their appearance with the meticulousness of a physician prepping for brain surgery. Too bad they're actually just trying to figure out what shoes will go best with their top.

Hello Libra...

Don't give us that doe-eyed "who me?" look. It's not going to work here. You may
have the rest of the world fooled into believing your helpless maiden act, but we
know the truth. You're not the unassuming, impartial ditz that you pretend to be.
In reality, you're a calculating game-player who hangs about on the sidelines and waits
until a winner is declared, then pretends you were with them all along. Your legendary
indecision comes less from wanting to be "fair" than it does from an intense desire
never to miss out. Your air-headed sign would rather spend its life floating from shiny
object to shiny object than get bogged down by things like "commitment"
and "loyalty." But hey, at least you're pretty.

DATES
September 23–
October 22

SYMBOL
Scales

RULER PLANET
Venus

ELEMENT
Air

MODALITY
Cardinal

OPPOSING SIGN
Aries

MORTAL ENEMY
Capricorn

PET PEEVES
Fighting, ugly décor,
binding contracts,
being left out

5 NOTORIOUS LIBRAS

Glamorous Libras certainly have some glitzy names in their ranks, from Serena Williams to Bruce Springsteen, but the sign is perhaps better represented by these equally eye-popping but slightly more notorious names:

1 **F. Scott Fitzgerald (September 24, 1896):** American novelist famous for *The Great Gatsby*. He pulled inspiration (and exact dialogue) from his glamorous wife Zelda's diaries before eventually leaving her in a psychiatric hospital.

2 **Bonnie Parker (October 1, 1910):** American bank robber who followed her partner Clyde Barrow into a life of crime in pursuit of money and fame. They even posed for pictures—rifles and all.

3 **"Squeaky" Fromme (October 22, 1948):** Attempted assassin and "Manson Family" member. She was sentenced to life in prison in 1975 for attempting to assassinate US President Gerald Ford.

4 **Kim Kardashian (October 21, 1980):** Trendsetting reality star who skyrocketed to fame with a *special* tape after humble beginnings as Paris Hilton's best friend and closet organizer.

5 **Richard III (October 2, 1452):** The final Yorkist king of England who was portrayed as a hunchbacked tyrant by William Shakespeare in his eponymous play. Many believe Richard may have ordered the deaths of his two young nephews to keep his crown.

Libra in a nutshell

Ditz, air-head, lightweight—these are all words you've probably heard used to describe you, Libra. And those are the people who are being nice. In reality, your charismatic sign is a master manipulator who only plays dumb in order to shirk responsibility. The ultimate people pleaser, your sign loves to tell people what they want to hear while keeping your true feelings a mystery. Libras are often called the Zodiac's "peacemakers," which may sound like a good thing, but we know it comes from a deep-seated and singular obsession with maintaining the appearance of tranquility, whether it matches reality or not. You'll do everything in your power to placate those around you in an effort to maintain "good vibes," even if it means completely changing your opinion to fit in with whoever you're talking to. This makes you a master of first impressions, as you're able to charm just about anyone with a glance. But that impression wears off quickly on your second meeting—and third, and fourth—when you reintroduce yourself and reveal you're blissfully unaware that you've ever met. No wonder you've had to perfect the art of the childish giggle and endearing "Oopsies!" You need it.

INDECISIVE

Even the most generous astrological breakdown will mention Libra's indecisiveness. You spend your life in a constant state of FOMO (fear of missing out). When faced with a decision, you'll procrastinate and vacillate, totally immobilized by the fear of what you'll miss from choice A if choice B goes forward. Libra's enemy is the buffet line. You'll literally starve in the face of a feast because you can't decide which entrée to sample first. This inability to make a choice is only amplified when it comes to interpersonal disputes. Friends know better than to try and pin you down on an opinion. You're a master of evasion and will use every trick in the book to avoid being cornered into taking a firm stance—from flirting, to pouting, to straight-up lying.

SHALLOW

Libras are the epitome of style over substance as they are only concerned with how things appear on the surface. So long as things seem beautiful and tranquil at first glance, they can hardly be bothered with digging deeper to discover how things actually are. Libra is represented by the scales, which gives the appearance of fairness and equilibrium. Whether or not that's really the case is none of Libra's concern. You are a master at sweeping dust and grime under the rug before guests arrive, then getting distracted by your own reflection and forgetting the dirt was ever there to begin with.

JUDGMENTAL

Is it any wonder a sign that's wholly concerned with appearances judges them so harshly? Whoever said not to judge a book by its cover clearly never met you. As far as Libra is concerned, the cover is all that matters. Every new person you meet gets the once-over from your exacting eye, and you will make a mental note of each and every hair that's out of place. Your singular obsession with beauty means you harshly judge any person, place, or thing that you find unsightly or plain. Diamonds really are Libra's best friend. The shinier, the better.

Libra placements

Sparkly Libra tends to command the attention of everyone in the room, so if you've got it as one of your "big three" there's no way you won't see its influence shining through. Here's a surface-level understanding of what Libra means for your birth chart. That's all they really care about, anyway.

VENUS IN LIBRA

Venus is Libra's ruling planet, so anyone who has their Venus in Libra is basically Aphrodite incarnate. Beautiful, selfish, and fully capable of starting the Trojan War on a whim, then turning around and acting like it was all Helen of Troy's fault. Your flirtatious romantic magnetism will mean many champions would happily die for a chance at your hand. Unfortunately for poor Achilles, he doesn't realize your irregular attentions are a bigger threat to his well-being than that heel will ever be.

LIBRA RISING

Got Libra as your rising sign? Then the world likely sees you as a social-climbing, ditzy flake who'd rather spend all day making inconsequential small talk than express an opinion or go deep on a topic. Sure, this can mean they also see you as fun and easy to be around—a total lack of substance will do that—and you're always invited when it's party time. But when a friend is in need of an honest opinion or deep discussion they'll scroll right past your name and onto someone they can actually trust to keep it real.

MOON IN LIBRA

A Libra moon's thoughts are simple: me, myself, and I. Consummate navel-gazers, a Libra moon means your interior life is concerned with yourself, your goals, your reputation, and pretty much nothing else. You're constantly calculating how to impress those around you, and will gladly change key parts of your personality to make this happen. This can often leave you feeling unmoored and directionless, since you're continually changing course to suit wherever the wind blows. At least you're charming!

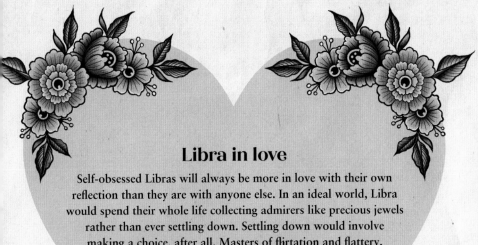

Libra in love

Self-obsessed Libras will always be more in love with their own reflection than they are with anyone else. In an ideal world, Libra would spend their whole life collecting admirers like precious jewels rather than ever settling down. Settling down would involve making a choice, after all. Masters of flirtation and flattery, Libra has an innate sense of how to beguile anyone and everyone with just one glance. Lovers will be dazzled by your ability to stare deeply into their eyes. What they don't realize is you're actually just checking out your own reflection in their irises.

SINGLE LIBRA

A single Libra is never really single; they're just floating blissfully through a state of noncommitment with a host of potential suitors. Your indifferent sign loves to live in the "What are we?" phase of a relationship, and will grow frustratingly evasive any time their partner tries (and fails) to demand an answer. The more they push, the more cold and heartless Libra becomes until they pull the ultimate move in the Libra arsenal: disappearing without a word. Shiny, transparent, and lacking in substance—is it any wonder Libra is the Zodiac's ultimate ghost?

LIBRA IN A RELATIONSHIP

It takes a determined person indeed to actually pin a Libra down to a commitment, usually via a steady stream of gifts and praise. Libras are high-maintenance partners who want to be treated like a housecat, pampered, petted, admired, and with no expectation they'll provide anything in return. No matter how "committed" your relationship appears, you'll always have one foot out the door, constantly scanning the horizon for a better option. Just as you were won over by gifts and admiration, so you can be quickly lost the moment a shinier object comes along. No wonder you've developed such an impressive collection of engagement rings. They just look so pretty on your finger!

Most compatible

Libra + Sagittarius

Air and fire generally make a great combination, so it's no surprise that Libra's best match is a Sagittarius. Both signs share an interest in being social, and Sagittarius's sense of humor will ensure all their conversations stay exactly where you like them: totally unserious. Archers love the thrill of the chase, meaning they'll actually find your indecisiveness and constant will-they-won't-they-ing attractive. As an added bonus, Sagittarius's carefree nature means they won't take it personally when Libra goes back on their word or refuses to commit, which is pretty much a prerequisite for anyone who wants to make it work with the master of scales.

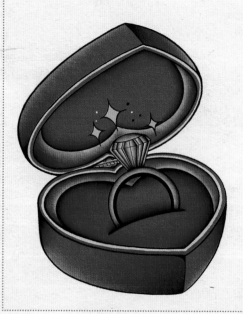

Least compatible

Libra + Virgo

These two perfection-oriented signs may find themselves initially attracted to each other, as Virgo will appreciate Libra's flawless outward appearance and Libra will appreciate Virgo's spotless surfaces (all the better for seeing their own reflection). That initial attraction will quickly wither, however, once you dig a bit deeper and find two diametrically opposed worldviews that lead to feelings of frustration and betrayal for Virgo and dismissive disinterest from Libra. Virgo's obsession with commitment and literal interpretation of promises and opinions (you know, they expect you to stick to them) will repel Libra, who hates being called to account for anything, especially their own opinions.

Libra + Aries

Aries' direct and confrontational vibe is simply too much conflict for light and breezy Libra. While you may initially love the adoration Aries pours on you during the courtship process, that feeling will quickly sour when Aries' jealousy and your conflict avoidance finally meet. The moment Aries realizes how many other admirers their flirty Libra keeps in tow, they'll be ready for a fight. Unfortunately for them, Libra sees even the slightest hint of a conflict as their cue to leave—usually without saying so much as a goodbye.

Libra + Libra

How can two navel-gazers even look up long enough to notice each other? A Libra will never be able to provide another Libra with the constant stream of adoration they require. They are both too busy looking in the mirror to realize their partner is even there. But it's the communication issues that will really do this couple in as neither partner will be capable of telling the other how they really feel, leading to a lifetime of long-simmering resentments and passive aggression. These two won't trust each other either, and for good reason. They know from experience just how easy it would be to convince their faithless partner to stray. Probably because they both already have.

LIBRA AT WORK

Lazy Libra knows how to appear busy when the boss comes around, but a brief glance at their computer screen will show that the "work" they've been "so busy" with all day was actually an online shopping spree. Libra's ultimate job would be something between a trophy wife and a courtesan, and they tend to view their job as a way to bide time until their meal-ticket reveals itself. Libra, your charming, easygoing nature often makes you a favorite with coworkers—until they need you to finish a task or give an opinion. Libras will worm their way out of ever delivering a verdict, even if that means leaving important tasks in permanent limbo. When workplace tensions finally bubble to the surface, you'll find Libra hiding in the break room hoping no one notices they've been playing both sides all along. In the event that you are the one in the hot seat, you'll bat your eyelashes, self-deprecate, and even unleash a flood of crocodile tears to make sure your poor HR rep can hardly remember why they called the meeting in the first place. Mission accomplished!

LIBRA IN THE FAMILY

As the family's Libra, you're definitely the one person everybody gets along with… but only because they don't know how you actually feel about anything. You're definitely the one that can be counted on to diffuse any family reunion flare-ups or placate that uncle at the dinner table. What nobody realizes is the Miss. Nice Niece act is all a ploy to make sure that once inheritance time comes around your name is at the top of everyone's list. Nobody knows this better than your siblings, who learned long ago that while you may swear up and down you'll help keep them out of trouble, you'll be singing a very different tune once your parents actually walk into the room. Your penchant for people pleasing is always at its peak when mom and dad are around. When tensions get too high, you revert to Plan B: avoidance. You have absolutely no problem skipping a holiday (or seven) if it means you'll be able to avoid a tough conversation.

LIBRA AT HOME

Beauty-obsessed Libras love nothing more than to decorate a space to their exact tastes and specifications, then to show off their handiwork via a series of lavish parties. As far as Libra is concerned, they are the definitive voice when it comes to art, music, and design, and they're basically doing the world a favor by inviting those with inferior taste over to see how it's really done. This makes you the ultimate silent critic any time you step into someone else's space, as you cannot help but make note of every outdated furnishing or—worse yet—slightly crooked wall art. Home is all about creating an environment of peace and symmetry for you, Libra, which is why you cannot abide a noisy neighbor or unkempt lawn. While you'd never confront them in person, you have no problem wielding the power of your neighborhood homeowners' association to keep the rest of your block in line, then serenely feigning ignorance when the nice old lady across the street asks why she's suddenly being fined for an "eccentric mailbox" violation.

LIBRA AND TRAVEL

Libra may seem like an easygoing travel companion, but anyone who has actually traveled with you knows the truth: holidaying with Libra is infuriating. While you may claim you have no opinion on accommodations, restaurants, and the itinerary, your travel companions will quickly realize that's not the case when they get a glimpse of your sourpuss face the moment you see something that's not to your liking. Even worse, you'll make sure the entire group wastes valuable sightseeing time hemming and hawing over every possible decision, from where to eat to what useless trinket to buy at the gift shop. You make friends wherever you go, which sounds nice enough. What people don't realize is that your "friendly" demeanor is also coupled with a complete lack of discernment when it comes to pickpockets, ne'er-do-wells, and scammers. One minute you're having the nicest chat with a too-friendly tour guide outside the Louvre, the next minute you're at the embassy trying to figure out where everyone's passports have gone. I guess that's just what you get for traveling with the Zodiac's ultimate air-head!

The two sides of Libra

It may surprise you to hear that Libra is one of the masculine signs of the Zodiac—probably because they wield their feminine wiles like a weapon of war. With that in mind, it should come as no surprise that within every Libra there is a dark masculine and dark feminine side just waiting to get out.

LIBRA DARK MASCULINE

Insecure, unreliable, and insensitive—when a Libra wakes up on their dark masculine side of the bed they embody all three. They're the type to make a date, confirm multiple times, then abruptly cancel at the last minute, even though they know the other person is already on their way.

LIBRA DARK FEMININE

A Libra that's expressing their dark feminine side may come off as bemused and empty-headed, but that's actually just an act. Dark feminine Libras are master manipulators who will do anything to get their way. Except, of course, actually telling someone what it is they want. Instead, they'll lay out a series of traps—I mean hints—for their unsuspecting partner to pick up on and see if they pass the test. Unfortunately for everyone involved, they rarely do.

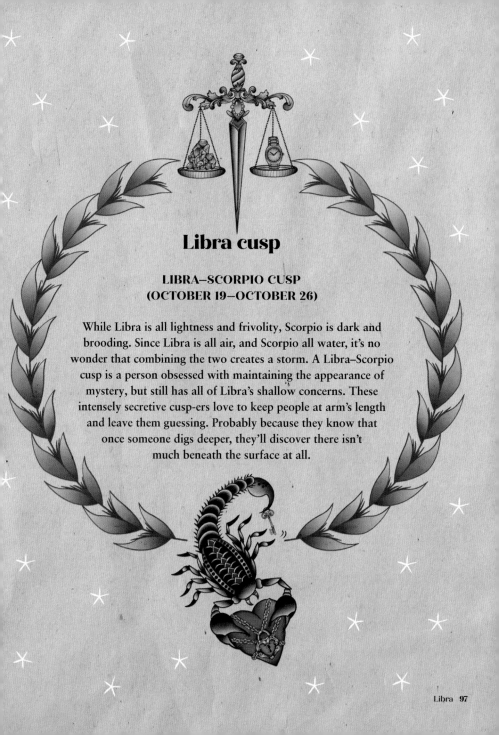

Libra cusp

LIBRA–SCORPIO CUSP
(OCTOBER 19–OCTOBER 26)

While Libra is all lightness and frivolity, Scorpio is dark and brooding. Since Libra is all air, and Scorpio all water, it's no wonder that combining the two creates a storm. A Libra–Scorpio cusp is a person obsessed with maintaining the appearance of mystery, but still has all of Libra's shallow concerns. These intensely secretive cusp-ers love to keep people at arm's length and leave them guessing. Probably because they know that once someone digs deeper, they'll discover there isn't much beneath the surface at all.

Hello Scorpio...

Your sign often gets a bad rap—and that's exactly how you like it. It's not hard to write about your dark side, considering it's the only side you've got. We'd call you an evil mastermind, but you'd probably take it as a compliment. There is no secret too salacious, no act too depraved, or torture too twisted for your ruthless sign to enjoy. In fact, you love nothing more than to watch other people squirm. A spiteful master of mind games, you use cruelty and intimidation to make sure no one gets close enough to see who you really are: a deeply insecure child in scorpion's clothing. Luckily, thanks to your noxious personality, nobody ever wants to.

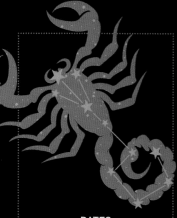

DATES
October 23–
November 21

SYMBOL
Scorpion

RULER PLANET
Pluto

ELEMENT
Water

MODALITY
Fixed

OPPOSING SIGN
Taurus

MORTAL ENEMY
Pisces

PET PEEVES
Small talk, air-heads,
canceled plans,
broken promises

5 NOTORIOUS SCORPIOS

All Scorpios aspire to fame and it's little wonder there are so many names to choose from. Your ruthless sign wants notoriety by any means. Here's a sample of the Scorpios who attained your sign's ultimate goal: infamy:

1 Marie Antoinette (November 2, 1755): The last Queen of France who had a love of finery and was insensitive to the problems of her people. She was executed at the height of the French Revolution.

2 John Gotti (October 27, 1940): American gangster and head of the Gambino crime family in New York City, famous for being one of the most powerful and ruthless crime bosses of all time.

3 Larry Flynt (November 1, 1942): American publisher who founded *Hustler* magazine and three pornographic news channels. His obsession with notoriety led him to push the envelope, including publishing nude photos of Jacqueline Kennedy sunbathing in 1975.

4 Christopher Columbus (October 31, 1541): Italian explorer who "discovered" the New World by stealing land from the native population. His exploration took him across the globe and led to the decimation of several indigenous societies.

5 Kris Jenner (November 5, 1955): "Momager" of the Kardashian clan, Jenner successfully managed the lives of her entire family leading to a popular meme declaring, "The devil works hard, but Kris Jenner works harder."

Scorpio in a nutshell

Not gonna lie, Scorpio, we're a little scared to roast you, knowing the pleasure you take in plotting revenge, but your tactics of intimidation won't work here. The Zodiac truly enters its villain era with you, since you love nothing more than scaring the pants off everyone you encounter. Your brooding, sex-obsessed sign is known for its unparalleled ability to make others feel uncomfortable, and there is no taboo that's too hot for you to touch. You've perfected the art of the menacing glare, which you gleefully employ on anyone who tries to get too close. Whatever friends you have know much better than to try and probe too deeply into your interior life, despite the fact that you're always pressing them to divulge their deepest, darkest secrets for your unholy collection. If someone does make it past your hard exterior and into your inner sanctum, they'll soon notice that the doors have locked behind them. You see those closest to you as possessions to be jealously guarded at all costs, and will keep them close by force if necessary. We'd say life with Scorpio is "'til death do us part," but you probably have more than a few tricks up your sleeve to ensure you'll still be able to get in touch from beyond the grave as well.

POSSESSIVE

Let us guess, Scorpio, your first word was "mine." As the most possessive sign in the Zodiac, once you get your hands on something you are never letting go, no matter how hard it may struggle against your constrictor's grip. This possessiveness also makes you intensely jealous. You have no problem going from zero to green-eyed monster the moment you feel that someone is encroaching on the territory you've claimed. Stage-five clinger? Lovers and friends wish you were that lax. You're more like a stage ten, and will lie in wait to lash out in private the moment you feel that their attentions are divided. How dare your BFF be caught texting another friend in your presence! As far as you're concerned, you should be the only number on their phone.

SECRETIVE

Scorpios love nothing more than collecting other people's secrets, but that shouldn't fool others into thinking you'll ever divulge one of your own. Scorpios love to maintain an air of mystery at all times, and would much rather leave a series of tantalizing breadcrumbs about their "dark" past than reveal themselves to another person. In your twisted mind, the truth makes you vulnerable, which is something your sign can never abide. People confide their secrets to you because they know you'll keep them... until they cross you, that is. Then, you'll use everything in your power to exact your revenge—the slower and more painful, the better. As much as you love exploring everyone else's dark underbelly, you protect yours with the viciousness of a cornered scorpion. Anyone who gets close can expect to feel your sting.

POWER-HUNGRY

Scorpios are known for their lust for power. Unfortunately for the rest of the world, you tend to define "power" in the most Machiavellian terms possible. Fear and intimidation are the name of your game, and you have no problem being ruthless or downright cruel to get what you want. Sure, you've mastered the art of subtle manipulation, and really love the feeling of intellectual superiority it can provide. But when that doesn't work, you're not above beating your foes into submission and will happily employ the most dastardly tactics imaginable in your quest for world domination.

Scorpio placements

If you've ever wondered why people's hair stands on end any time you're around, having Scorpio at the top of your chart is probably the reason. Unsettling Scorpio doesn't need to be your sun sign to creep in and spread darkness throughout your chart. Here's what to expect if you've got the scorpion as any of your "big three."

MOON IN SCORPIO

Having your moon in Scorpio means your internal life is spent living on the dark side of the dark side. Your inner monologue is mainly concerned with plotting, manipulation, and pouring over a treasure trove of dark secrets. You're that friend who can bust out an encyclopedic knowledge of serial killers and their methodologies and is always up for a seance (and knows how to perform one). We wouldn't be surprised to hear most of your thoughts are spoken in tongues. Frankly, just thinking about them scares us.

SCORPIO RISING

Got a rising sign in Scorpio? No wonder people tend to run away screaming whenever you arrive. Your public persona is that of a dark, intimidating, super-human who may or may not have made a deal with the devil to gain unearthly powers. Sexy, spooky, and suspicious, people may be slightly intrigued by your mysterious aura, but their terror and the unease you inspire will keep them away.

VENUS IN SCORPIO

Be honest, you only bought this book to try and find your perfect match, didn't you? Scorpio Venuses are obsessed with love and finding a soulmate. They dive heart-first into all of their love affairs and have no problem exploding with passion the moment they feel a spark. The instant a romantic connection is made, you're all in, and expect nothing less than the same devotion in return. In short, don't be surprised if you have a shotgun wedding—or several—in your future.

Scorpio in love

The line between love and hate is never blurrier than in your twisted heart, Scorpio. On the one hand, your passionate sign loves love and is constantly on a quest to find its perfect partner. On the other, your deep sensitivity and jealous tendencies mean you can easily turn your lovers into enemies the moment they cross one of your many invisible lines. Scorpios need intensity in all aspects of their life, so it's no surprise that they're attracted to intensely sexual, highly emotional relationships. It's almost as if your entire sign read *Fifty Shades of Gray* and thought, "Challenge accepted."

SINGLE SCORPIO

Sex-obsessed Scorpios have no problem enjoying everything the single life has to offer. Your astronomical levels of lust and constant need to push boundaries in the bedroom borders on nymphomania, and you have no problem spreading your passions far and wide. You also have no problem spending a wild night baring your soul (and a few other things) with a stranger, only to follow your passions to another bedroom the next night. Given how protective you are of your own heart, you would think that you'd be less careless with other people's. Unfortunately, for your growing list of one-night stands, that's not the case.

SCORPIO IN A RELATIONSHIP

Unlike their scorpion mascot, Scorpios mate for life. Your possessive and obsessive sign loves to pursue deep connections and sees all partners as a potential soulmate. Unfortunately for them, your definition of "soulmate" means that two become one, even at the expense of your own independence. Your secretive nature can also lead to trust issues, and any perceived slight will cause you to lash out. You love to set secret tests for your partners to assess their loyalty, then subject them to a lengthy silent treatment when they fail. In the bedroom, your lusty sign loves to push boundaries, and you're going to need a partner that's along for the—ahem—ride. An immunity to rope burn is also preferred.

Most compatible

Scorpio + Cancer

Scorpios aren't just looking for a soulmate; they're looking for a partner in crime. Luckily, they've found it in their fellow water sign, Cancer. Cancer will have no problem giving everything to their Scorpio partner and will gleefully answer all of Scorpio's probing questions. Plus, this introverted pair will love nothing more than to spend long nights at home together planning their future...and plotting their revenge.

Least compatible

Scorpio + Leo

When water meets fire there are bound to be problems. There's no compromise when it comes to this power-hungry pair. Both sides will always want to be right and would give up the relationship rather than give up control. Jealous Scorpio will hate Leo's attention-grabbing tendencies, and naturally extroverted Leo will loathe Scorpio's need for one-on-one time. Even though Scorpio's sexy, mysterious vibe and Leo's shiny personality may lead to an initial attraction, this mismatch will be pretty hard to overcome.

Scorpio + Libra

Light and bubbly Libra loves to live a life of peace and tranquility, which sounds like nothing so much as a snooze-fest for intrigue-obsessed Scorpio. While Libra strives to keep all their social interactions pleasant and conflict-free, Scorpio loves nothing more than to make it weird and watch the mess unfold. Libra's changeability will always be at odds with Scorpio's need for stability, and their trust issues will be forever triggered by the Libra partner's flirty nature. Scorpio will find themselves forever chasing their flighty Libra partner, leading to intense frustration…and more than a few voodoo dolls.

Scorpio + Aquarius

Heady Aquarius is all intellect, while Scorpio is all emotion. These two may initially bond over their shared hatred of conventionality, but their differing worldviews will inevitably lead to conflict. Aquarius is always trying to make the world a better place, while Scorpio would much rather spend time probing the dark corners of humanity's basest pursuits. Independent-minded Aquarius will never give Scorpio the undivided attention they need from a partner, and Aquarius will grow frustrated with Scorpio's need to turn every conversation toward emotions. While they may respect each other's complete disregard for the ordinary, these two are better off as friends.

SCORPIO AT WORK

Your ideal career would either be as a secret agent or a police interrogator. Barring that, ruthlessly moving your way up the corporate ladder while silently sabotaging your coworkers' ambitions will have to do. Your covetous sign cannot abide being an underling, meaning you quickly develop a deep and abiding hatred for any "boss" or "manager" that stands in your way. You'll stop at nothing until your name is the first one on the masthead, not because you actually care about success in your field, but because you crave power over others. In fact, you spend half your work hours secretly searching for other jobs while plotting ways to take down the company with your exit. But while you may have absolutely no loyalty, you also have no patience for treachery from a colleague. Your scorpion-like tendencies are on full display the moment you feel wronged in the workplace, and you have no problem lying in wait and collecting secrets until the ideal time comes for you to strike. Did your "work bestie" actually think they'd get a promotion over you? All it'll take is one anonymous email to the boss detailing their deepest, darkest secrets to make them realize your work friendship was as fake as their resume.

SCORPIO IN THE FAMILY

While most people spend their energy trying to avoid family conflict, you love nothing more than to stoke it. You know exactly which button to push to send every one of your family members over the edge. And you'll gladly push— preferably moments after dinner is served at a holiday. Despite your devil-may-care attitude, your intense jealousy means you also want to be the favorite, and you have no problem manipulating emotions behind the scenes to make that happen. You know exactly what to do to pit family members against each other while using your collection of family secrets as an insurance policy to ensure nobody will ever do the same to you. While you love nothing more than to find out everyone else's business, your secretive nature means you never let your guard down long enough for them to get to know you in return. Even with family, your true feelings remain hidden behind a labyrinth of insurmountable walls, leaving you feeling eternally lonely and your family members with an unshakable feeling that they'll never know what's really going on behind your sly smile. Probably because it's the truth.

SCORPIO AT HOME

The ideal Scorpio abode is more like a dungeon than a living space. The shades are always drawn, both to discourage visitors and to keep prying eyes from seeing the depraved acts going on inside. Scorpios thrive on darkness and will want that to be reflected quite literally in their décor. As far as you're concerned, there's no such thing as too much black—from the sheets to your clothes to the color you splash on the walls. The few guests you do allow into your den of depravity shouldn't be surprised to see occult items strewn about, or sexually charged art hanging in the communal areas, just daring them to ask what it is you get up to in your off hours (not that you'd ever tell). Your gothic heart will be reflected in the materials you bring into your home, and you're no stranger to metallic furniture or stone floors. As for the thermostat, you like to keep your home roughly the same temperature as your heart—just above freezing.

SCORPIO AND TRAVEL

Scorpios like to travel alone—preferably to a dangerous location where they don't speak the language. Vacationing Scorpios eschew tradition and are way more interested in seeing a city's seedy underbelly than the typical sites. While Scorpio's travel companions will spend their days taking in the usual tourist traps, you choose to sleep the day away and save all your energy for sampling the destination's nightlife. Any attempt from fellow travelers to impose a plan will be met harshly, since you'd much rather explore based on intuition alone. Scorpios prefer to travel on the edge of danger, instead of in the lap of luxury, and love nothing more than arriving at the dingiest hostel in town with only a few coins and an outdated travel book, then seeing what happens. For some that sounds like the premise of a horror movie, but for you it's the perfect vacation itinerary.

The two sides of Scorpio

Scorpio is one of the Zodiac's feminine signs, but that's not to say this sign doesn't have two dark sides to choose from. These sex-obsessed water signs tend to be fluid in their gender expression, but here are the two poles every Scorpio has inside.

SCORPIO DARK MASCULINE

Lavish displays of passion and romance are accompanied by intense bouts of possessive jealousy for Scorpios that are situated in their dark masculine. A Scorpio that's expressing its masculine side does everything with a hint of violence and intimidation, and there's no telling when they might lash out. Thought the average Scorpio was guarded? Just wait until you meet one that's expressing its dark masculine side. They're way more likely to be hiding a secret family than to show vulnerability with the ones they love.

SCORPIO DARK FEMININE

Scorpios love to live in the feminine, which is their natural state of existence. Dark feminine Scorpios are sensual to the point of making others feel uncomfortable, which only turns them on even more. On the flip side, Scorpios that are expressing their feminine side are also more likely to be vindictive, and have never felt a grudge they couldn't hold on to for dear life. They know how to take down anyone with a cruel word—or even just a single icy glance.

Scorpio cusp

SCORPIO–SAGITTARIUS CUSP
(NOVEMBER 18–NOVEMBER 24)

The Scorpio–Sagittarius cusp is called the Cusp of Revolution, and there's no convention these cusps won't challenge. Sagittarius's vicious wit mixes with Scorpio's love of watching people squirm in these folks, giving them an almost supernatural ability to cause discomfort. There's no fight from which these cusps will back down. It's good you've inherited Sagittarius's near-pathological independence, since you'll often find yourself alone.

Hello Sagittarius...

Life is just one big joke to you, isn't it? Well, we're deadly serious when we say you're the Zodiac's obnoxious know-it-all. You may fancy yourself a philosopher, but in reality you're a blowhard doomed to repeat the same stories and jokes for the rest of your life. It's honestly impressive the way you can go on and on, blissfully unaware that you're not impressing anyone at this party—which you totally crashed, by the way. Your foolhardy sign lives its entire life in search of fun, burning through connections and guzzling up experiences at a pace so quick you never really enjoy them. You may rack up some good stories along the way, but you'll spend your whole life cycling through people to hear them.

DATES
November 22–
December 21

SYMBOL
Archer

RULER PLANET
Jupiter

ELEMENT
Fire

MODALITY
Mutable

OPPOSING SIGN
Gemini

MORTAL ENEMY
Scorpio

PET PEEVES
Rules, emotions,
predictable situations,
sensitive people

5 NOTORIOUS SAGITTARIANS

Archers spend their whole lives hunting excitement, so it should be no surprise that the pursuit has turned up more than a few unsavory characters, including these five infamous folk:

1 Patrizia Reggiani (December 2, 1948): Italian socialite and matriarch of the Gucci family who had her ex-husband shot after he divorced her for another woman.

2 Lucky Luciano (November 24, 1897): American gangster who helped develop the American organized crime syndicate in the 1930s. He was convicted of running a prostitution ring in 1936 and fled to Cuba, where he continued to serve as a mob leader until his deportation to Italy in 1946.

3 Emperor Nero (December 15, 37 CE): Notorious Roman emperor known for executing his enemies, including his own mother, and for his persecution of early Christians. His reign was marked by tyranny and extravagance, and for the great fire that destroyed much of Rome in 64 CE.

4 Pablo Escobar (December 1, 1949): Colombian drug lord and leader of the Medellín Cartel, Escobar amassed massive wealth as the so-called "King of Cocaine." He was killed by police after escaping house arrest at the elaborate mansion prison he built for himself known as "La Catedral."

5 Mary, Queen of Scots (December 8, 1542): The life of this queen of Scotland was marred by a series of disastrously bad decisions. She was eventually executed after being caught plotting against her cousin, Queen Elizabeth I.

Sagittarius in a nutshell

Party's over, Sagittarius. Your gluttonous sign lives for excess. Your sex, drugs, and rock 'n' roll ethos might seem exciting from the outside, but you'll turn up empty-handed when it comes to the things that really matter in life. Introspection? Nope. Commitment? Nada. Intimacy? Not so much. You're represented by the archer, meaning you love to portray yourself as a straight shooter. But it's easy to take shots when you keep everyone at a distance. That's why you burn through relationships well before any form of real attachment can be developed. Friends know they can always count on you to get the party started, but they also know they'll always come second to your never-ending pursuit of a good time. You'll spread their secrets far and wide if they make for a good story, and have no qualms using your sharp wit to stab them in the back if it'll help you feel superior. Ultimately, in the hunt for true friendship, you archers rarely hit your mark.

RECKLESS

You take devil-may-care to a whole new level, Sagittarius, and often end up paying the price. Your lust for novelty, and obsession with spontaneity, often blind you to any potential consequences your actions may bring, landing you in more than a few sticky situations. Your impulsive sign is totally incapable of thinking ahead, and will blindly follow your every whim only to end up shocked at the wreckage later. Your long-suffering parents are used to late-night phone calls from you pleading with them to bail you out of your latest easily avoidable emergency. You try to play this trait off as a hilarious quirk of your spontaneous lifestyle, but after the third phone call from jail most people will discover you're actually the one thing you hate most in the world: thoroughly predictable.

TACTLESS

One of your favorite mottos is "truth hurts." Unfortunately for those around you, an archer's truth typically comes in the form of a shot through the heart. Your zero-filter sign never stops to think about the effect your words may have on others, and is often blithely unaware of the hurt feelings you create. Your complete lack of tact means you often leave people feeling offended, which you quickly write off as just another example of someone being "too sensitive" for your rapier wit. But how many "too sensitive" people does someone have to meet before they take a look at how their own behavior affects others? For undiplomatic archers, the limit does not exist.

OBNOXIOUS

Loud, garish, ham-fisted Sagittarius loves nothing more than to take over an entire room with their explosive energy. You may think this makes you the life of the party, but more often than not you're just annoying everyone. Your over-the-top behavior guarantees that the attention is on you at all times, and you can hardly conceive of a world in which that's actually a bad thing. Your clueless sign has never met a party it couldn't crash, and will typically just assume you were left off the guest list by accident. Who wouldn't want to hear you loudly recounting your lengthy stories while everyone else is trying to sing "Happy Birthday?" You simply can't imagine.

Sagittarius placements

Just as the obnoxious personality of Sagittarius takes over every room it enters, so the archer takes over every birth chart it appears in. You may think you dodged a bullet avoiding Sagittarius as your sun sign, but if you've got this domineering dandy as any of your "big three," you're in for some problems—not that you'd ever stand still long enough to realize it.

VENUS IN SAGITTARIUS

Those with their Venus in Sagittarius are frenzied romantics who love to sweep someone off their feet only to leave them without a leg to stand on. These "free-love" advocates would have done well in the swinging sixties, but struggle with monogamy and settling down. Lucky for you, we hear polyamory is on the rise…

MOON IN SAGITTARIUS

Sagittarius moons think about the future so much they're incapable of living in the moment. Their obsession with the next best thing means they're totally lacking in introspection, and their thoughts move at such a rapid pace they never stop to appreciate what they have. People can tell you spend every conversation thinking about what you're going to say next instead of listening. That's probably why they rarely bother to tell you anything of particular note.

SAGITTARIUS RISING

If you've got Sagittarius as your rising sign it means the world sees you as an over-the-top extrovert obsessed with having a good time. They probably think of you as the ultimate party-hopper, good for getting on a VIP list, but far too impulsive and narcissistic to be trusted. When others talk, they can literally feel you not caring. Your habit of scanning the room to see if someone more exciting has arrived doesn't help either.

Sagittarius in love

Those born under the sign of Sagittarius spend their entire life chasing excitement, and what is more exciting than love? Until the other person starts making demands, of course. You love the start of relationships, but are easily spooked the moment your beloved starts to have expectations of their own. Fiercely independent Sags will do anything to maintain their autonomy, and lash out at anyone who they feel is trying to take it from them. It's probably a good thing you love your freedom so much—you may very well end up alone.

SINGLE SAGITTARIUS

Single Sags love to burn through hot-and-heavy flings at a frenetic place, then leave their one-night-only partner with their head still spinning. Your declarations of love may be true in the moment, but the feelings tend to burn out by morning—just like the candles you lit to set the mood. In many ways, Sags are designed for the single life as they don't want to be tied down by anyone and can't bear the idea of a life without as many sex-capades as possible. In the bedroom, you may think of your "wham, bam, thank you ma'am" style of lovemaking as passionate, but it can often end up coming off as frantic to those on the—ahem—receiving end of your frenzied advances.

SAGITTARIUS IN A RELATIONSHIP

Sags naturally want to roam free, so in order to settle down you'll have to find the right jockey for your inner wild horse. Sags often make very callous partners as their brutal honesty and independence can mean they often have a hard time taking their partners' feelings into account. You take very little seriously, Sagittarius, and see everything as merely an intellectual exercise, meaning emotions, especially those of other people, are rarely at the forefront of your mind. You seek novelty over stability and would rather have a series of passionate affairs than a committed relationship. Good thing you're not one to get lonely.

Most compatibile

Sagittarius + Leo

For the rare Sagittarius that actually does want to settle down, your best match is fellow fire sign Leo. "Look-at-me" Leo knows how to keep someone's attention, even yours. Their fun and flirty extroverted side means life will always be exciting, plus they're way too obsessed with themselves to bother with putting rules and restrictions on their partner. So long as you shower them with passionate kisses and admiration when you are around, they won't be worried about what you get up to when you're not. A willingness to take lots of cute-couple photos is also a plus.

Least compatible

Sagittarius + Scorpio

Sagittarians and Scorpios may find themselves initially attracted to each other, thanks to Scorpio's mysteriousness and Sag's air of danger, but the relationship will fizzle out the moment Scorpio's possessiveness comes out to play. Sagittarius's inability to take emotions seriously will enrage their Scorpio partner, while Scorpio's jealousy and need for reassurance will only push Sag farther and farther away. Ultimately, this pairing is way more likely to end up in lifelong enmity than become a perfect match.

Sagittarius + Taurus

Boring, steady Taurus will never be able to keep a Sagittarius's attention long enough to sustain a relationship. Sure, Sag will be happy to hop into bed with Taurus every once in a while after they hear about their notorious sexual prowess, but bulls will never be able to keep archers' attention for more than a few hours. Taurus is just far too stable for chaos-loving Sag. As for Taurus, the moment Sagittarius turns up late for a dinner date and causes them to lose a reservation, thoroughly turned-off bulls will be out the door. At least neither of them will feel the need to say goodbye!

Sagittarius + Cancer

Cancer is a homebody. Sagittarius is an adventurer. See the problem? Restless Sagittarius will never sit still long enough for cozy Cancer's liking. Sag's complete lack of tact will never fly with sensitive Cancers, who are known for taking everything personally. But the real death knell for this match is their differing worldviews. Sagittarians are bon vivants who love life and all it has to offer, while Cancers are naturally gloomy pessimists who would rather spend the day at home with their feelings. These two can barely see eye to eye, let alone go through life side by side.

SAGITTARIUS IN THE FAMILY

When was the last time you called your grandmother, Sagittarius? Actually—scratch that—have you ever called her? Flighty Sagittarius can hardly be bothered to pick up the phone, meaning most of your family members tend to learn about your major life events through social media. As with all your other relationships, you're happy to show up for the family reunion (especially if there's free food and drink), but your unsentimental sign is not one to put maintaining familial connections at the top of their to-do list. When you do show up for the odd holiday or birthday party, your lack of tact usually puts you at the center of whatever squabble is threatening to ruin the day for everyone. You just can't help but ask Aunt Marge about her divorce proceedings, or point out cousin Katie's new nose. The more boring or mundane the family affair becomes, the more likely you are to light little fires for the pure amusement of watching them burn. Who says pop-pop's retirement party can't double as an episode of *Family Feud*?

SAGITTARIUS AT WORK

Working 9–5? No thanks. Your novelty-loving sign chafes against even the most mild routine, and you'd much rather juggle five jobs that you're mediocre at than settle in and do one job well. Coworkers know the only thing they can count on you to show up for is happy hour, and your ability to turn even the tamest office holiday party into a debauched bacchanal is the stuff of office legend. Your love of hearing yourself talk is on full display in an office, which you view less as a place of work and more as a venue for you to test out your best jokes and stories. Meetings, in particular, are unbearable with you. While you may see your colleagues as a captive audience, they'll feel more like hostages, forced to listen to your constant interruptions when they really just want to go to lunch. Not only are Sagittarians completely lacking in professional decorum, but they'll also lose their temper at anyone who tries to impose the rules, even if that person is the boss. In fact, the harder the powers-that-be try to rein you in, the more outrageous your behavior will become. That's probably why your list of firings could fill a novel, while your list of professional references barely fills a page. Oh well, you are a fire sign, after all.

SAGITTARIUS AT HOME

Home? You mean that place you store your underwear between trysts? Any address associated with wanderlusty Sagittarius is usually more of a pit stop than a home base. For you, "home" is just a place where people can send your mail—and even then, you're way more likely to let it pile up on the kitchen counter than you are to actually open it. Sagittarius never wants to feel like they've settled down, and what's more settled than a permanent residence? You'd much rather spend your life couch surfing than put down roots. You're always on the move—literally—which is why your "home" is filled with half-unpacked boxes that will stay that way until you relocate again. Your fridge is a resting place for decaying takeout and your bedroom is almost as messy as your love life. Your extroverted sign is always on the go and barely ever spends any time at home, so you really can't understand why your landlord is so angry you forgot to pay the rent (again). Chill out, bro. You'll get to it next time you're around—probably in a month or two.

SAGITTARIUS AND TRAVEL

Risk-chasing Sagittarius is the most travel-obsessed sign in the Zodiac. In your ideal world, you'd never have time to unpack your carry-on between trips. You're a self-proclaimed travel expert and bring a "Sagittarius-knows-best" vibe to any group trip you attend, regardless of how much you actually know about your destination. This makes you an extremely condescending travel partner, despite the fact that you're also the person most likely to completely disregard important cultural norms about dress, behavior, and speaking volume. (You only have one setting: loud.) You're that tourist who will pretend that they speak the language when actually you're just parroting phrases you learned from a guidebook with an accent so wrong you accidentally end up saying something offensive. But hey—if you end up with a black eye, that's no problem. Nothing bores you more than a trip that goes according to plan. Anyone who joins you on one of your jaunts should be prepared for you to roll up to your flight five minutes before takeoff, coffee in hand and a phone with one percent battery, totally unphased that you almost ruined the trip for everyone. What? You'll just sleep at the airport and fly out the next day. Not like you haven't done it before…

The two sides of Sagittarius

Sagittarius is a masculine sign, but that doesn't mean archers don't have both masculine and feminine sides to contend with. Like every other sign, Sagittarius has a dark masculine and a dark feminine side that they can tap into on any given day. Here's what to watch out for from both.

SAGITTARIUS DARK MASCULINE

When Sagittarians are expressing their dark masculine side, their recklessness comes to the fore even more than usual. These impulsive hotheads have no problem starting fires just for the rush of watching other people put them out. Dark masculine Sags will bulldoze their way into any conversation just to hear themselves talk, and love to initiate a battle of wits with anyone who dares try to get a word in for themselves. Unfortunately this verbal sparring can turn into physical fights faster than you can say "devil's advocate."

SAGITTARIUS DARK FEMININE

Sagittarians expressing their dark feminine side love to spend a night out on the town flirting with everyone they come into contact with, regardless of that person's feelings or relationship status. They'll happily break up a marriage just for the story, and have no problem inviting multiple suitors to the same party so they can watch them all duke it out for their affections. Those on the receiving end of their coquettish ways may be left with the distinct impression that these Sags get off more on the drama than they do on the romance. They'd be right.

Sagittarius cusp

SAGITTARIUS–CAPRICORN CUSP
(DECEMBER 18–DECEMBER 24)

A mutable fire sign meets a cardinal earth sign with these cusp-ers, meaning they are constantly fighting an internal battle between Sagittarius's reckless thrill-seeking and Capricorn's prudent practicality. This toxic pairing creates someone who is hyperfocused on themselves and their own ambitions with a complete lack of sensitivity to how their single-minded pursuit of success might affect those around them. In short, you're the ultimate evil genius.

Hello Capricorn...

Sorry to interrupt your workflow with something as trivial as introspection; we promise this won't take long. Your stuffy, spiritless sign is represented by a goat—probably because of your unique ability to destroy any playground you come upon. Your "all-work-and-no-play" sign simply doesn't have time for things like "fun" or "enjoyment." You're far too busy methodically working your way through your checklist for world domination. Yes, that's right, we know about your plan. Others may think you're simply another cog in the corporate wheel, but we know better. Underneath your unassuming demeanor and buttoned-up shirt is a ruthless, power-hungry tyrant carefully working through a 100-step plan to impose your will on the masses.

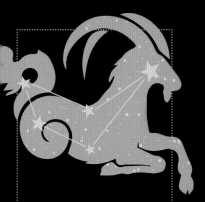

5 NOTORIOUS CAPRICORNS

Capricorns seek power, not the limelight, so will fly under the radar as second-in-command, but this hasn't stopped your sign producing internationally recognizable figures like Catherine Middleton and Dolly Parton—or these famous names:

1 Al Capone (January 17, 1899): Prohibition-era gangster prominent in organized crime as the Chicago Outfit boss. He ruthlessly organized the infamous St. Valentine's Day Massacre, but was only charged with tax evasion before spending the rest of his life in Alcatraz.

2 Marie Lafarge (January 15, 1816): French husband-killer convicted of using arsenic to poison her spouse in 1840 (the first conviction due to forensic toxicological evidence), she wrote her memoirs in prison, doggedly proclaiming her innocence.

3 J. Edgar Hoover (January 1, 1895): American FBI director who launched witch hunts against so-called communists, "deviants," and civil rights leaders, all while allegedly hiding his own "deviant" lifestyle.

4 Edgar Allen Poe (January 19, 1809): American writer whose macabre works put the "goth" in "Gothic." His methodical mind led him to invent the detective story, but he is best known for works involving untimely deaths, tell-tale hearts, and prophetic ravens.

5 Howard Hughes (December 24, 1905): Wealthy American manufacturer, aviator, and film producer better known as a recluse. Severe obsessive compulsive disorder meant he spent much of his later years in exile in luxury hotel rooms across the United States.

DATES
December 22–January 19

SYMBOL
Sea goat

RULER PLANET
Saturn

ELEMENT
Earth

MODALITY
Cardinal

OPPOSING SIGN
Cancer

MORTAL ENEMY
Aquarius

PET PEEVES
Unserious people, broken protocols, wasted time, children

Capricorn in a nutshell

You may think we're here to call you boring, Capricorn, but we know that's all an act. In fact, we'd actually say that you're the most interesting sign of all. Sociopaths are interesting, after all. Your conservative, no-frills appearance masks an inner tyrant quietly biding their time until they can seize power and rule with an iron fist. Your unsuspecting demeanor is just a front for your true self: a petty, cruel absolutist who spends their gloomy life silently convinced that they're better than everyone around them. Sure, there are plenty of other signs that see themselves as perpetually in the right, but they lack the stamina needed to actually enforce their views on the world. Not you. Your domineering sign is a master of quiet influence, and you'll stop at nothing until you're calling the shots. Friends—to the extent that your work schedule will allow you to have friends—know that they will always come second to your ambition, especially if they have nothing material to bring to your master plan. Who has time for things like weddings and birthdays when there is work to be done?

RIGID

If you don't bend you'll break...unless of course you have a will of steel. Capricorns know there is exactly one optimal way to do things, and it's the way they've always been done. The ultimate disciplinarian, your sign has no patience for loosened restrictions, lax behavior, or—horror of all horrors—casual Fridays. Your complete and total adherence to protocol makes you every boss's dream and every coworker's nightmare, as you clock and report even the slightest deviation from the norm to the appropriate authorities. Your religious devotion to the status quo makes it almost impossible for you to take in new information or consider alternative paths for doing things, and you have no problem expressing your disdain for anyone who colors even slightly outside the lines. The 1950s called. They want their mentality back.

PETTY

Anyone who thinks there are things too small to be complained about hasn't met you, Capricorn. Your petty sign is the master of making mountains out of molehills. You can hardly go out to eat without sending at least something back to the kitchen because you found the dish to be too salty/not salty enough/too cold/too hot. In social interactions, there's no grudge too small for you to hold onto, and you're notorious for taking unnecessary jabs at anyone who crosses you (or dared to cross you ten years ago). You take any opportunity you can to express your disapproval, which is constant. Have you ever considered a career as one of Bravo's Real Housewives? You'd fit right in.

CHEAP

You may describe your financial philosophy as "sensible" or "frugal," but anyone who has ever had to split a check with you would probably describe it a bit differently. You're cheap. Your Scrooge-like sign looks for every possible opportunity to pinch pennies, even if it comes at the expense of those around you. You'll happily deduct ten percent off a waiter's tip for inefficient water delivery and have no problem subjecting your travel companions to the most barebones accommodation if it means saving a buck. For you, the least expensive option is always best and you'd rather live a life of Spartan austerity than ever be caught spending a penny more than is absolutely needed. This makes you an excellent money manager for any business you're a part of, but an absolute nightmare when the office tries to plan anything fun. Who needs balloons on their birthday? The unencumbered air is free!

Capricorn placements

Low-key Capricorn may not be the star of your birth chart, but it doesn't need to be. Capricorn would much rather assert its subtle influence via some of the lesser placements until it brings you to heel over the course of years. Suddenly, you look around and your life is all Capricorn, whether you want it to be or not.

MOON IN CAPRICORN

Your moon sign represents your internal life, and when your moon is in Capricorn it means you spend all your energy trying to find new ways to be productive. You have no time to spin your wheels on intellectual pursuits, frivolous hobbies, or fruitless emotions. Instead, you are singularly focused on the next step you need to take to make it to the top. Some may say you're quiet, but really you're just biding your time. Soon they'll see... they'll all see!

VENUS IN CAPRICORN

Those with their Venus in Capricorn are looking for one thing and one thing only: commitment. Summer flings, one-night stands, and brief flirtations are of no interest to them as all of that is simply a waste of time. They conduct their romantic life like a series of job interviews for the role of "life partner," all the way down to checking a potential partner's LinkedIn before making a date. Nothing says romance like a well-formatted resume.

CAPRICORN RISING

If you've got Capricorn as your rising sign it means the world sees you as a stuffy sourpuss who only cares about work. Some may say you're just shy or stoic, but in truth the perception tends to match reality. You *are* a stuffy sourpuss who only cares about work. There are only so many times you can turn the dinner conversation to annual expense reports before you stop getting invited out by anyone.

Capricorn in love

Is a Capricorn ever actually in love? Or are they only briefly allowing themselves to feel a love-like emotion because getting married is part of their ten-year plan? Either way, potential partners should know not to expect a shower of romance from you. Your practical sign sees love and marriage as something to cross off your to-do list in lifelong pursuit of the status quo. Anyone who hopes to be brought on at Capricorn Inc. will need to present their resume and qualifications before being considered for the role. If they're a fit, they'll hear from you in three to five business days. If not, they shouldn't expect to hear anything at all, since you've already moved on to more suitable candidates.

SINGLE CAPRICORN

Single Capricorns are not overly preoccupied with their single status. They're married to their work as it is. If they are dating, it's more because that's just what people do than it is the result of a genuine desire for romantic companionship. This will be immediately apparent on a first date, which will always feel to the other person more like a job interview than a night out. You're not one to waste time and will want to hear how they answer your list of necessary preliminary questions before you agree to go on a second date—or even have a second drink.

CAPRICORN IN A RELATIONSHIP

Any potential partner for your high-achieving sign will have to be okay with always coming in second to work in your ambitious heart. If they can handle the late nights and constant office talk, you will agree to provide them with a stable yet emotionally distant companionship that will technically meet all of the requirements of a romantic relationship. They shouldn't seek out lavish displays of emotion, but they can expect that the bills will be paid and the house will be clean. Once the appropriate relationship milestones have been met, they can look forward to an uninspired proposal, traditional wedding, and subsequent production of 2.5 children as per the most recent census. Well, it worked for your grandma!

Most compatibile

Capricorn + Scorpio

Once a Capricorn has reached the stage in life where they have decided a partner is necessary to achieve the remainder of their goals, they should set their sights on a Scorpio. You may think traditionalist Capricorn and boundary-pushing Scorpio would never work, but in this case water and earth mix to make a mud that both partners can wallow in. Capricorns are loyal and stable partners, meaning Scorpio will never have to worry about the trust issues that plague their other relationships. Scorpio will love the fact that under Capricorn's mild-mannered persona there is an immense and slightly terrifying dark side to explore, and introverted Capricorn won't have any problem spending time in Scorpio's lair divulging dark secrets. Unless there's work to be done, of course.

Least compatible

Capricorn + Aquarius

Free-thinking Aquarius and status-quo obsessed Capricorn see the world through two very different lenses. Capricorn will find themselves forever frustrated by their Aquarius partner's inability to commit to anything, especially a conventional job. Meanwhile, Aquarius will tune out the moment they hear the words "ten-year plan." The end goal of a Capricorn relationship is a classic wedding—frills and all—while an Aquarius would be much happier eloping to Vegas while wearing their favorite Halloween costume. It's just not a match, is it?

Capricorn + Libra

Noncommittal Libra will drive Capricorn crazy, and Libra will grow to resent their Cap partner's constant attempts to hold them to what they say. Capricorns are ultra-direct and simply cannot understand Libra's passive-aggressive communication style, or why their opinion keeps changing based on who they're talking to. Capricorn is also one of the only signs that is totally immune to Libra's flirtatious charms, as they're much more concerned with substance than style. Meanwhile, Libra will head for the hills the moment they realize their no-frills partner doesn't even own a full-length mirror for them to primp in.

Capricorn + Leo

Leo and Capricorn may initially find themselves attracted to each other for their social status, but the relationship will quickly dissolve over one simple snag—they'll never be able to agree on what to do. Leo is the ultimate extrovert and will want to show off their six-figure Cap partner as much as possible at parties, dinners, and networking events. Understated Capricorn will find all of Leo's bragging obnoxious and would much rather spend a quiet evening at home gearing up for the workday ahead. They don't need a gloating partner to pump them up. Unfortunately for them both, gloating is what Leo loves best.

CAPRICORN AT WORK

Capricorn at work? Don't you mean their happy place? Capricorns live for work and work to live. To you, the office is the one place where the world actually makes sense. It's the one place where your ceaseless ambition doesn't make you a sociopath, it makes you a boss. Or at least, it will once you complete your ten-year plan to take over the company and run it the way it actually should be run. You love efficiency and cannot stand to see valuable resources wasted on slacking employees, office happy hours, or—worst of all—team-building activities. You get to the office early every day just to make everyone else feel late, and your coworkers know you'd ban all chitchat and smiling if you could. You bring a distinct "not-here-to-make-friends" attitude to the workplace that makes you the perfect person to heartlessly conduct a mass layoff on the boss's behalf. Colleagues see you as the ultimate brown-noser, always sucking up to the boss and acting as their little informant on the floor. You never question authority, mainly because you intend to be the authority one day. Your introverted sign hates the spotlight, so your ultimate goal is always to be the power behind the frontman. That way, someone else can take the blame (and the fall) while you act as the quiet puppet master, holding the strings and the power.

CAPRICORN IN THE FAMILY

Quick question, Capricorn. How many times have you heard the phrase "You're not my dad!" at a family event? Too many to count? That's what we thought. Capricorn is the ultimate father figure, regardless of where they actually fall in the family tree. You're a natural provider who relishes in doling out resources to help your bloodline thrive. But those who accept your assistance should beware. These handouts often come with a closed fist and tight leash, as you'll also expect anyone who takes your help to abide by your rigid standards. Your house, your rules. Capricorns see the success of their family members as a reflection of their own achievements, and you have no problem making your disapproval known to any artsy cousins who are still "figuring things out." Your tough-love approach to familial relationships means you're often the one the younger generation dreads being seated next to at family events, especially if they know their latest report card isn't up to snuff. But hey, at least you can always be counted on to execute your great-great-grandma's pecan pie recipe to perfection!

CAPRICORN AT HOME

Some people fill their home with signs that read "live, laugh, love" or "gather." Your home says "Don't touch." Stuffy, conservative Capricorn wants their living quarters to feel more like a museum than a home. As far as you're concerned, a house is a place for people to display their heirlooms and refuel before returning to work. Capricorn's décor is stiflingly old-fashioned, either passed down in their family by generations or acquired at an estate sale. You couldn't care less about trends, and guests who step over a Capricorn's threshold often feel like they've been transported back in time. So what if your wallpaper is from a previous century? If it worked for the Victorians, it'll work for you. The Capricorn home checks all the boxes of a classic domicile, but lacks any of the warmth to make it feel really lived in—probably because it isn't. If home is where the heart is, then your home is the office building where you spend the majority of your day. You just maintain a separate residence because sleeping in your cubicle is against company policy.

CAPRICORN AND TRAVEL

"Capricorn" and "travel" are two things that generally do not mix. If you can be persuaded to take your vacation days, you'd much rather spend that time at home, contemplating when you can get back to work again. In your mind, travel is a frivolous, expensive endeavor only undertaken by dilettantes who are not currently in the midst of a methodical plan to take over the world. If you do travel, usually at the behest of a partner or family member in desperate need of fun (Why? You don't know), you'll budget the entire thing down to the penny, leaving no room for spontaneity or reckless spending. There will be no five-star dinners or trips to the shopping district when you're around. If you do plan something to do on your trip, it's probably because you were able to finagle a discount or find a coupon. You'd fly in the cargo hold if it meant a cheaper ticket, and refuse to stay anywhere but the most budget accommodation. If you end up with bedbugs, then that's just another sign that you never should have left home to begin with.

The two sides of Capricorn

Despite their dad-like energy, Capricorn is one of the Zodiac's feminine signs. That said, a dark masculine and dark feminine side exists within every Capricorn, silently plotting until they can make their intentions known. Any Capricorn can find themselves grappling with one of these two identities on a given day. Here's how to spot which one has taken over.

CAPRICORN DARK MASCULINE

A Capricorn that's situated in its dark masculine takes their "emotionally distant father" dial and cranks it up to an 11. Hard-nosed, domineering, and totally unconcerned with anything that is not a verifiable fact, dark masculine Caps often come off as rude or cold. Probably because they are actively choosing to be rude and cold. You can attempt to tell them about your day if you want, but they'll most likely just be watching your mouth move while they think about something at work.

CAPRICORN DARK FEMININE

Detached dad, meet overbearing mom. Capricorns situated in their dark feminine are perpetual cynics who aren't happy keeping their worldview to themselves. Instead, they try to impose their way of thinking on everyone around them, believing wholeheartedly that if the world could only see things their way, it would be a much better—and more organized— place. They treat everyone like children in need of a firm hand and have no problem dispensing advice to those who they feel need it, which just so happens to be everyone they've come into contact with.

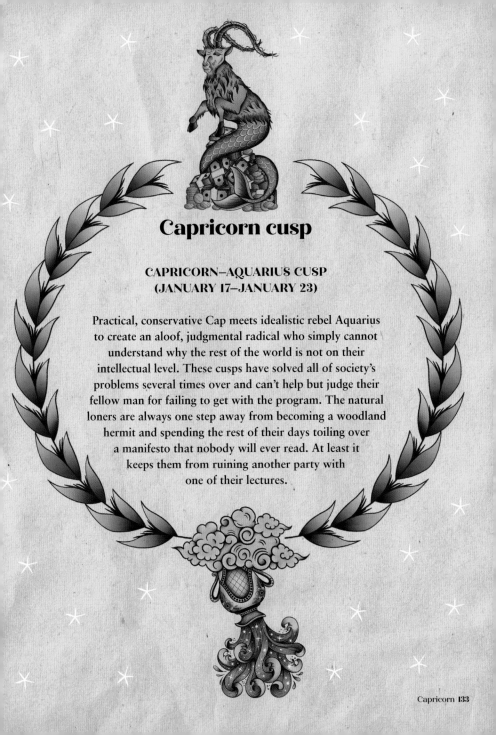

Capricorn cusp

CAPRICORN–AQUARIUS CUSP
(JANUARY 17–JANUARY 23)

Practical, conservative Cap meets idealistic rebel Aquarius
to create an aloof, judgmental radical who simply cannot
understand why the rest of the world is not on their
intellectual level. These cusps have solved all of society's
problems several times over and can't help but judge their
fellow man for failing to get with the program. The natural
loners are always one step away from becoming a woodland
hermit and spending the rest of their days toiling over
a manifesto that nobody will ever read. At least it
keeps them from ruining another party with
one of their lectures.

Hello Aquarius...

Or whatever other-wordly greeting you would prefer. As the Zodiac's resident space alien, we're sure you'd be more than happy to hear all about how "weird" and "non-traditional" you are. But that's not what we're here to talk about. Instead, let's talk about how your obsession with aloofness and rebellion keeps you trapped in an ice palace of your own making. It's easy to look down on others from your satellite on Mars, but real changemakers are the ones who come down to earth and get their hands dirty. How many hermits do you know who actually publish their manifesto?

5

NOTORIOUS AQUARIANS

Aquarians love to point to the changemakers and artistic innovators in their sign, like Oprah Winfrey and Harry Styles, but that's not all this Zodiac sign has given us. It's one thing to be offbeat, but these five infamous Aquarians are downright notorious:

DATES
January 20–February 18

SYMBOL
Water bearer

RULER PLANET
Uranus

ELEMENT
Air

MODALITY
Fixed

OPPOSING SIGN
Leo

MORTAL ENEMY
Pisces

PET PEEVES
Tradition, rules, people who say they're "not political," the status quo

1 Grigori Rasputin (January 21, 1869): Russian mystic who ingratiated himself with the Romanov family since he could magically "heal" the tsarevich Alexei's hemophilia. He survived many attempts on his life before being drowned in the Neva River. His influence over the royal family is thought a factor in the eventual Russian Revolution.

2 Elizabeth Holmes (February 3, 1984): Tech entrepreneur who claimed to have invented a device for multiple blood tests from a single finger prick. She was found guilty of fraud when it was discovered her device never worked and sentenced to 11 years in prison.

3 David Lynch (January 20, 1946): American filmmaker whose boundary-pushing work, including *Twin Peaks* and *Blue Velvet*, is known for its often disturbing imagery that can leave audience members feeling uneasy.

4 Lord Byron (January 22, 1788): English poet who enjoyed various scandalous relationships, including a rumored affair with his half-sister's daughter. One lovelorn ex described him as "Mad, bad, and dangerous to know."

5 Paris Hilton (February 17, 1981): American heiress to the Hilton hotel fortune, often regarded as the first "influencer." Her public behavior in the early 2000s made her a tabloid staple and led to run-ins with the law.

Aquarius in a nutshell

Aquarius loves its reputation as the Zodiac's rebel, but riddle us this: does it really count as being a rebel if your "rebellion" is so predictable? At a certain point your loved ones all learn to roll their eyes at your eccentric style and constant chafing against the status quo. If you're able to maintain any loved ones, that is. Constantly analytical and aloof, you rarely put in the emotional work necessary to maintain real connections. Instead, you'd much rather keep other humans at arm's length, observing them as if you're an extraterrestrial tasked with reporting back to the mothership about human life. And sure, you have lots of ideas about how to make this strange planet called Earth a better place, but they usually stay just that: ideas. Your independence-obsessed sign is totally incapable of asking for help to put your plans into action, and will never admit when someone else has knowledge or expertise that exceeds your own. Instead, you'll spend your entire life with your head in the clouds, pontificating about what the world could be if you got your way. Sadly, everyone else is just too boring and pedestrian to understand the true genius behind "no-pants Wednesdays." Dullards!

DISTANT

So close, yet so far away. For as much as you claim to be a humanist, connecting with other humans one-on-one isn't really your strong suit. Instead, Aquarians like to keep everyone in their life at a distance. They prefer to keep their conversations intellectual, not emotional, and will lean heavily on their talent for sarcasm the moment anyone tries to get close. With your arms crossed and your head in the clouds, you laugh in the face of anyone who tries to get you to engage with human emotions. While you love thinking about the big picture, you can often find it hard to connect with what is happening right in front of you. But how exactly do you plan to change the world if you refuse to actually live in it?

PROUD

It's one thing to believe in yourself. It's another to believe in only yourself. Aquarians live their lives with their nose in the air, totally assured that they are better in all things. It's part of the reason why you're so committed to marching to the beat of your own drummer—you're convinced that they're playing the superior tune. For as much as you hate rules, you are totally rigid in your adherence to your own ideas about how things should be. You would rather die than ask for help because that would mean admitting there might be someone else on the planet whose intellectual capabilities match your own. If it's true that pride goeth before a fall, then you'd better keep a first-aid kit handy.

LONER

Who needs other people when you've got all your big ideas to keep you company? Aquarius is the Zodiac's lone wolf—and you like it that way. Nothing gives you a bigger thrill than to spend an entire party standing in a corner looking interesting. If someone is smart enough to come over and ask you a question, then good for them. They've passed your test and have earned the right to be regaled with your latest idea for how to achieve world peace (usually without being able to get a word in themselves). If nobody approaches and you spend the whole party in stoic silence, so be it. You didn't even want to come, anyway. You have no problem flying solo because you see it as a testament to how unique you really are. But is it really your "uniqueness" that keeps people away? Or do you just give off bad vibes?

Aquarius placements

High and mighty Aquarius doesn't need to be your sun sign to exert its influence. This air sign can blow anyone in its idealistic direction, especially if it appears in another one of your birth chart's "big three." Eccentric weirdos just know how to make a splash that way.

MOON IN AQUARIUS

If your moon is in Aquarius, then your emotional life is...thoroughly unemotional. You'd much rather spend all your time pouring over big ideas than big feelings. Unfortunately for you, the distance you create with yourself also creates a distance with others, who can't help but feel there's a lot hiding behind your detached expression. No wonder so many of your closest relationships only exist online.

VENUS IN AQUARIUS

Those with their Venus in Aquarius thrive in long-distance relationships. Physical touch is not your love language, and neither is showering your beloved with attention every second of the day. You don't need much from a partner and want someone who won't expect much from you in return. Meeting up once a month to howl at the full moon is fine with you.

AQUARIUS RISING

The good news? If you've got your rising sign in Aquarius, you want the world to see you as different—and they do! The bad news? It's in less of a "cool rebel living their best life" kind of way and more of a "creepy loner who lives in the woods" kind of way. Maybe it's your distant stare. Maybe it's your general "alien on a business trip" vibe, but either way, other people feel like something is just a bit off about you. If only they knew you come in peace! Sort of...

Aquarius in love

Partnership does not come naturally to you, Aquarius. You'll always be more in love with your own ideas than another human. When you do find someone whose freak flag flies as high as yours, you'll still only open up once they've passed through your gauntlet of mind games, thought experiments, and riddles. More often than not, the person will just give up rather than suffer through another lengthy text exchange about a hypothetical scenario when all they asked was where you want to go for dinner.

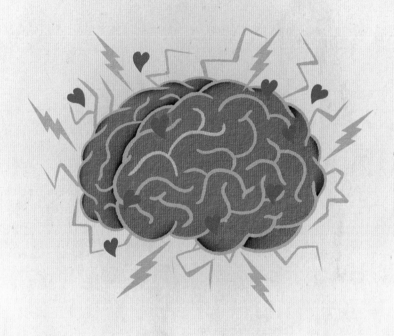

SINGLE AQUARIUS

A single Aquarius has usually been that way for a while and barely even noticed. You prefer to spend your life alone contemplating what an ideal match would be like if—and that's a big if—you were to engage in one. You're the definition of a sapiosexual, aka someone who has to be attracted to a person's mind before they could possibly consider a romantic relationship. Until such a mind-connection is met, you're happy to get your rocks off through sex parties and online encounters—the less "vanilla" the better.

AQUARIUS IN A RELATIONSHIP

Thanks to your feelings of superiority, you tend to be highly selective when considering a potential partner, and will only agree to enter into something as normative as a committed relationship with someone who you feel can match your wit and intellect. Outward appearances mean very little to you. In fact, you're much more likely to fall for the unconventionally attractive weirdo everybody tells you to stay away from than you are the local heartthrob. You know the girl in the YA novel who falls madly in love with the pale quiet guy despite the fact that she's 99.9 percent sure he's a vampire? She's definitely an Aquarius.

Most compatibile

Aquarius + Aries

Want to actually make a relationship work? Find yourself an Aries. The doer and the thinker meet with this pair, as each fuel each other's best tendencies. Detached Aquarius is far too above-it-all to trigger Aries' competitive streak, while Aquarius's constant stream of eccentricities will be just enough to keep Aries' wandering eye interested. Aquarius will love the fact that passionate Aries will always have the enthusiasm to put their ideas into action, and Aries will love that flighty Aquarius will never get angry when they burn out and move on to the next thing. This is a partnership made in half-finished-project heaven. Just don't ask them to actually plan a wedding.

Least compatible

Aquarius + Cancer

Differing worldviews, values, and needs make this match a nearly impossible one to make work. Emotional Cancer wants a partner who will stick around all day and wallow in feelings. Then you have heady Aquarius, who finds nothing so boring as discussing base emotions and finds the needs of others totally stifling of their independence. One is a gloomy pessimist primarily concerned with the here and now, the other is a heady optimist with their eyes permanently focused on the horizon. It's hard to imagine these two having a successful conversation, let alone a relationship.

Aquarius + Virgo

An Aquarius–Virgo relationship can best be categorized as a hamster wheel of criticism. Virgo will criticize Aquarius for their messiness and unpredictability and Aquarius will hammer Virgo for their obsession with perfection and order. Virgo will hate the way Aquarius constantly questions their way of doing things, which they consider to be the product of perfectly sound logic and research. Meanwhile, Aquarius will be left feeling like their every move is being noted by a live-in hall monitor. Relationships are built on mutual affection, not judgment.

Aquarius + Pisces

Sentimental Pisces is one of the worst possible matches for heady Aquarius, as these two will simply never be able to give each other what they need in a relationship. Pisces will take all of Aquarius's sarcastic remarks to heart, and Aquarius will never even try to understand why Pisces' feelings are so perpetually hurt. A notorious grudge-holder, Pisces will build up a well of resentment for their Aquarius partner, while Aquarius will be so busy with their own thoughts they won't even notice anything is wrong. Eventually, it'll boil over into an epic Pisces meltdown—usually because Aquarius forgot to get Pisces a birthday present (again).

AQUARIUS AT WORK

The three favorite words of Aquarius: work from home.
You love nothing more than to toil away in solitude on your
latest project, and hate engaging in mundane office politics and
small talk. Your tech-obsessed sign loves to conduct all its business
virtually, away from the prying eyes and small ideas of your oh-so-
normal coworkers. Once you rise through the ranks to become the boss
yourself, employees know to expect you'll get totally derailed anytime
some shiny new piece of tech comes your way. You're all about innovation
for innovation's sake, and are perpetually chasing the next best thing, even
if the old way of doing things was perfectly fine. Your constant desire to be on
the cutting edge means you rarely stop to think about whether or not change is
necessary—just that it's available. This obsession with novelty means you often leave
projects half finished as you float from shiny new idea to shiny new idea. In meetings,
you love ideating endlessly over the big picture, but when push comes to shove you
just cannot bring yourself to dig into the little details that actually make the big picture
happen. As impressive as you are when you're standing on your soapbox, it doesn't
take long for coworkers, bosses, and clients to realize you're really just a lot of hot air.

AQUARIUS IN THE FAMILY

Every family has its eccentric, and Aquarius, that's you. You're that weird aunt/cousin/sibling who nobody really understands and never RSVPs to anything but always shows up (late) to tell everyone about their latest big idea, invention, or cause. It's not that you don't care about your family—in many ways you feel like they're the only ones who truly understand you—but you're not one to let it show. The only way for a family member to know you love them is if you let them talk. Thinking someone is smart enough to be listened to is the highest form of compliment from Aquarius.

Otherwise, you have no problem dominating the dinner table conversation with every "taboo" topic under the sun, from politics to religion to whether or not there is life on other planets. (The answer is yes, and you are their representative.) You love to pick out your stodgiest and most conservative family members, then keep pushing their ideological buttons until they eventually break. This tendency has put you at the center of more than a few holiday blowouts, but you don't mind. At this point your relatives know to duck for cover the moment you start "just asking questions."

AQUARIUS AT HOME

The Aquarius home cannot be constrained by the normal trappings of art and design. If you want to put a bed in the middle of a living room and a couch in your kitchen, then that's what you're gonna do. You don't care about things like "matching" and will use any color you want anywhere you want. Some people might need a seizure warning before walking through your door, but that's not your problem. If your guests don't find the décor overwhelming, the beeps and boops from your various machines might be the thing that sets them over the edge. Your tech-loving sign would live in a fully automated Smart House straight out of an episode of *Black Mirror* if they could. You love nothing more than to show guests the new computer you built, or how you can turn the lights on and off with a clap. And sure, maybe this means Big Tech can hear your every move, but as far as you're concerned that's just one more person to listen in on all your brilliant ideas.

AQUARIUS AND TRAVEL

Aquarians love to travel...alone. In fact, you'd love nothing more than to spend your days roaming to the Earth's most far-flung locations, making notes on your fellow man as a detached observer of the human condition. Those who try to organize travel with you will find that you cannot be constrained by things like "itineraries" or a "return ticket." You're much more interested in the locals than you are in your travel companions, and are prone to wandering off for hours, then turning back up at the hotel just when everyone was about to call the police. Friends and family know better than to expect to get a call or an update from you when you're abroad, as home is the last thing on your mind. In fact, you see every new place you visit as an exciting opportunity to become an expat. Why not? You're an outsider wherever you go anyway. There is no food too adventurous or custom too foreign for you to explore, and you will rebel against any tour guide or tourism board that tries to tell you what to do—even if it's for your own safety.

The two sides of Aquarius

Detached Aquarius is one of the Zodiac's masculine signs, but this does not mean they don't have a feminine side that they can tap into any time they want. Aquarius eschews anything like traditional gender roles and loves to live their life floating between masculinity and femininity as it suits them. Here's what to expect on a day when they are landing more to one side than the other.

AQUARIUS DARK MASCULINE

Cold, condescending, and emotionally unavailable—an Aquarius who woke up on the dark masculine side of the bed is the epitome of all three. They hardly have time for things as mundane as human emotion, and will rarely come down off their high horse long enough to consider what those on the ground have to say. Totally convinced of their own superiority, these loners would much rather spend the day wrapped up in their own thoughts than with another human. Some may say that makes them a robot. They'd take that as a compliment.

AQUARIUS DARK FEMININE

An Aquarius that's situated in its dark feminine side pushes back hard against any attempt by an outside force to impose its will, even if it's something as simple as a "no dogs allowed" sign outside a café. These thoroughly unpredictable menaces to society love nothing more than to show up late, wreak havoc, and leave without saying goodbye. The dark feminine Aquarius is all about shaking up institutions just to see if they hold, regardless of whether or not that shakeup is warranted or helpful. They're basically the prototype for the "manic pixie dream girl" that dominated 2000s rom-coms. Unfortunately for everyone, the schtick is a lot less charming in real life.

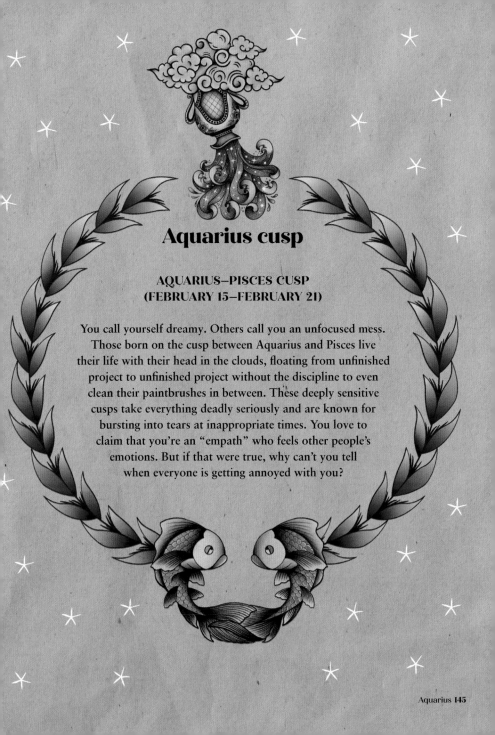

Aquarius cusp

AQUARIUS–PISCES CUSP
(FEBRUARY 15–FEBRUARY 21)

You call yourself dreamy. Others call you an unfocused mess.
Those born on the cusp between Aquarius and Pisces live
their life with their head in the clouds, floating from unfinished
project to unfinished project without the discipline to even
clean their paintbrushes in between. These deeply sensitive
cusps take everything deadly seriously and are known for
bursting into tears at inappropriate times. You love to
claim that you're an "empath" who feels other people's
emotions. But if that were true, why can't you tell
when everyone is getting annoyed with you?

Hello Pisces...

Of all the signs we've roasted so far, we're pretty sure you're the most excited to get to your chapter. Why? Because it means you get to engage in one of your all-time favorite activities: playing the victim. Poor, misunderstood Pisces can always find a reason to have their feelings hurt. So let's give you some. Your clingy, lazy, gullible sign is basically the poster child for willful naivete. You never seem to know anything about how the world works and love busting out your babe-in-the-woods act anytime someone (i.e. your boss) expects even a modicum of maturity or responsibility. You wear your guilelessness and sensitivity like a badge of honor, constantly lamenting the fact that the rest of the world can't be more like you. Luckily for you, being blissfully unaware of eye rolls is one of your superpowers.

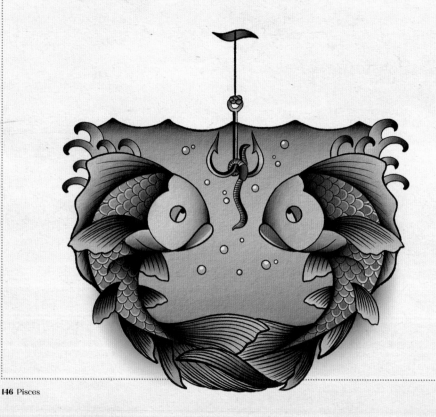

DATES
February 19–March 20

SYMBOL
Fish

RULER PLANET
Neptune

ELEMENT
Water

MODALITY
Mutable

OPPOSING SIGN
Virgo

MORTAL ENEMY
Capricorn

PET PEEVES
Awkward silences, know-it-alls, being asked an ETA, emotional distance

5 NOTORIOUS PISCES

Pisces love gushing about the creative titans in their artistic ranks, from Elizabeth Taylor to Steve Jobs, but this mercurial sign has a dark side better represented by these five notorious names:

1 Anne Bonny (March 8, 1697): One of the only known female pirates, Irish Bonny and her band terrorized the Caribbean until she was captured alongside fellow pirate Mary Read in October 1720. She and Read escaped death sentences by claiming to be pregnant. Bonny's true fate remains unknown.

2 Kurt Cobain (February 20, 1967): 1990s rocker credited with popularizing the Seattle grunge sound as the frontman of Nirvana. He struggled with addiction and tragically took his own life at the age of 27.

3 L. Ron Hubbard (March 13, 1911): Sci-fi writer who founded the Church of Scientology. The subject of numerous documentaries and exposés, many former members say it is actually a dangerous cult.

4 Patty Hearst (February 20, 1954): American heiress kidnapped by a guerilla group only to join their ranks and start robbing banks with them. She later claimed to have been brainwashed and received a presidential pardon for her crimes.

5 Joe Exotic (March 5, 1963): American zoo owner whose wild antics and love of collecting tigers were the subject of the Netflix documentary *The Tiger King*. He was arrested in 2018 for attempting to murder his rival, Big Cat Rescue owner Carole Baskin, and is serving 21 years in prison.

Pisces in a nutshell

Poor little Pisces. All you want is to be able to spend your days swimming from fantasy world to fantasy world in a state of blissful ignorance about the real world around you. You probably already know and love your reputation as the Zodiac's artistic soul, but what about your other claim to fame as the Zodiac's ultimate dilettante? Your moodiness is the stuff of legend, meaning you often go from being totally enthusiastic about an idea one minute to completely over it the next. Friends know to expect at least five potential versions of you to show up to any given event, several of which are in a state of emotional distress. You say you're just sensitive, but those who know you best realize you're also a spotlight hog who loves to use emotional outbursts to be the center of attention. And if anyone dares call you out on your woe-is-Pisces behavior? Bring on the waterworks—and the grudges. For someone so scatterbrained, you sure can hold on to your resentments. In fact, you're probably adding this book to your ever-growing list of personal grievances at this very moment. Sorry fishy. Didn't mean to ruffle your scales. It's just so easy...

LAZY

Pisces are often considered the old souls of the Zodiac, so it's no wonder they act as if they're already retired. Weak-willed Pisces will drop any task the moment they face the slightest hardship, and their work ethic is practically nonexistent. You would rather float along aimlessly going wherever the tide takes you than put forth even the slightest effort to change direction. In fact, just the thought of putting in effort has already left you feeling exhausted. You've never met a deadline you couldn't blow through, for no reason other than that you couldn't muster up the motivation to meet it. Pisces will always take the path of least resistance, even if it means they never quite get what they want. Luckily for you, your laziness means you never really want anything too deeply either.

CLINGY

If you look up the words "insecure attachment style" in the dictionary, you will probably find a picture of a Pisces. Pisces crave external validation. The closer you get to someone, the more constant praise and reassurance you'll need. For Pisces, every moment a text goes unanswered is another sign the recipient secretly hates them, and the only remedy for that is more text messages. Just ask your ex. If, of course, they haven't already blocked your number to stop the near-constant demands for "closure." What these exes don't realize is you've got no problem camping out at their favorite coffee spot for as long as it takes to "accidentally" run into them.

GULLIBLE

Some people might say Pisces is very trusting. We say Pisces is always one email scam away from losing their life savings. When it comes to red flags, your sign is essentially color blind. You love to believe the best of everyone and have no radar for deceit, meaning there is nothing you won't fall for. While at first this trait can seem kind of sweet, eventually your loved ones will grow tired of bailing you out of your latest totally predictable predicament. In an attempt to spare them, repeat after us: No one needs to talk to you about your car's extended warranty, a Nigerian prince does not need your help accessing his inheritance, and that person you haven't seen since high school's message about an "exciting opportunity to be your own boss" is not as good as it may seem.

Pisces placements

Not a Pisces sun sign? That doesn't mean you're out of the deep end. Pisces has a way of pulling you into its moody, mercurial tide from anywhere it appears in your birth chart, especially if it's one of your "big three." If you've always felt like a bit of an overly sensitive space cadet, you can probably thank your Pisces placements.

MOON IN PISCES

If you've got your moon in Pisces, your inner life is a fantasy world of your own design. People are probably used to having a conversation with you only to notice midway through that they've lost your attention to whatever elaborate hypothetical scenario your Piscean brain has conjured up. You're also super-sensitive and often find yourself taking on the emotions of others, aka hijacking their problems to make everything about yourself. Oops.

PISCES RISING

If you've got your rising sign in Pisces, then you are someone the world sees as deeply in need of a reality check. Consider this that check. You spend your life floating from unrealistic goal to unrealistic goal, with zero wherewithal to actually make them come true. Everyone can tell that your ideas are half-baked, but they also get the sense that you're way too sensitive to hear the truth. They're right.

VENUS IN PISCES

If you've got your Venus in Pisces, it means you love love. You're all about the thrill of romantic connection and spend your days fantasizing about your future soulmate. Unfortunately, your rose-colored glasses make it almost impossible for you to see red flags, meaning you often give your heart away to the wrong person and end up hurt. Your friends all told you that the DJ you met on vacation had bad vibes. You were just too love-drunk to listen.

Pisces in love

When it comes to love, Pisces only wants three simple things: constant praise, unwavering support, and everlasting gratitude. Emotionally dependent Pisces needs a partner that is comfortable being the center of their world and is willing to center their Pisces partner in return. Until you find such a person, you're more than happy to indulge in an intense string of fantasy relationships with individuals either real or imagined. You're basically the Zodiac's Snow White, mournfully singing "Someday My Prince Will Come" into a wishing well until the day your soulmate magically appears. It's a lovely dream, but you might find yourself waiting for a while.

SINGLE PISCES

Single Pisces is never really single. In fact, they've probably got multiple make-believe relationships that they are deeply invested in at any given time. Your high-powered imagination can't help but go into overdrive when it comes to your love life, meaning you leave every first date planning a wedding and wondering what your kids will look like. You catch feelings easily, and the intensity of your initial affection can often scare off a relationship before it even begins. This only serves to send you off on another string of fancies in which the person who rejected you shows up ten years from now—preferably at your wedding to a more attractive version of them—to announce they actually loved you all along. It happens in the movies!

PISCES IN A RELATIONSHIP

When Pisces falls in love, they fall hard. You quickly make your partner the center of your world, meaning you're often that friend who totally disappears the moment they get into a relationship. In return for your loving devotion, you expect your partner to shower you with a constant stream of praise and affection. Your need for external validation is never so intense as when you're in a relationship, and you are constantly on high alert for the first sign that your partner's affections might be waning. This insecurity only makes you cling harder, which can end up leaving your partner feeling smothered, so they push away. So you cling, and they push away. Which makes you cling, so they push away—and so on, and so on...

Most compatible

Pisces + Virgo

You may be thinking "messy Pisces and structured Virgo could never make it work!" But you'd be wrong. A Pisces + Virgo match is the perfect example of opposites attracting, as Virgo will love the "project" their chaotic Pisces partner presents, and Pisces will love Virgo's stability, commitment, and attention. Pisces lives in an imagined world, while Virgo is thoroughly reality-oriented, meaning that when these two get together big things might actually get done. Most importantly, Pisces' perpetual rose-colored glasses when it comes to romance makes them uniquely able to see Virgo's nitpicking for what it is: an expression of love.

Least compatible

Pisces + Libra

Noncommittal, self-centered Libra is basically a Pisces' romantic worst nightmare. Libras are far too cool and aloof to ever give Pisces the level of devotion they need. The lack of affection will activate Pisces' insecurities, causing them to cling to their Libra love for dear life. While Libra understands why Pisces would be obsessed with them (who isn't?), they'll always prioritize their independence over Pisces' comfort. These two may find common ground over their love of art and shiny objects, but that's where the connection ends.

Pisces + Gemini

Pisces will run into similar problems with noncommittal Gemini, with the added bonus that Gemini's charm will lead them on to think there really is something there. Pisces will spend their whole life chasing the fantasy of their relationship with Gemini, with Gemini dropping just enough affectionate breadcrumbs to string Pisces along for life. When Gemini inevitably drops them to pursue another (usually Aquarius), sensitive Pisces will be left with a broken heart and a grudge they'll hold onto for life. At least one part of this relationship was built to last.

Pisces + Sagittarius

Simply put, Sagittarius is just too mean and independent to make it work with a Pisces partner. Pisces' delicate self-esteem isn't built to withstand Sagittarius's wit and tactlessness, as they'll always take Sag's off-handed comments to heart. While Sag may love the fun, chaotic, artistic energy Pisces brings to life, they'll chafe at Pisces' constant need for validation and will see all of their attempts at closeness as an attack on their precious independence. These two may make great roommates or travel partners, but they're definitely better off remaining as friends.

PISCES AT WORK

"Work" and "Pisces" are two things that generally do not mix. You're just not someone who is built for traditional employment. Or any employment, really. In the workplace you thrive during a creative brainstorming session, but lose steam the moment it's time to put one of your big ideas into action. Instead of working, you spend most of your time wondering if your bosses and coworkers are mad at you, which in turn makes them mad at you because you haven't been working. Your sluggish sign is no stranger to being called into the boss's office to get put on a corrective course of action that does nothing to stem the flow of missed deadlines or half-finished projects. Coworkers like that you're always available for a good cry in the breakroom (unless you're already in there crying yourself), but know better than to come to you with anything involving the words "ASAP" or "by EOD." Those acronyms are simply not in the Pisces vocabulary. We'd say your best shot at a career would be something in the arts, but even Picasso had to actually produce a painting every once in a while.

PISCES IN THE FAMILY

Pisces loves to oscillate wildly between being the baby of the family and/or the wise elder. One minute you're dispensing sage advice to the younger generation about the nature of life, love, and creativity, the next you're crying at the dinner table because of an old sibling argument you can't let go of. You take familial love very seriously and can get guilt-trippy or needy when you feel like a member of the clan isn't pulling their weight. You're the first person to take it personally when someone opts to see their in-laws for the holidays or can't make the family picnic this year. Pisces also tend to suffer from a lack of boundaries with their family members, often sharing too much with the wrong people at the wrong time. This can be particularly difficult if you ever become a parent, as you tend to treat your kids like they're your friends and overshare. You also totally crumble when it is time for serious decision-making around things like finances or an elderly family member's health. When hard choices need to be made, you're nowhere to be found and will only show up again later when the decisions have been made to cry about how hard it all was for you.

PISCES AT HOME

When thinking about Pisces' home life, only one word comes to mind: chaos. Dreamy, artistic Pisces is someone who makes messes, not someone who cleans them up. Because of this, your home tends to be a shrine to all your half-finished projects and incomplete endeavors. Since your moods are so changeable, the idea of sticking to one color palette or décor style is typically out of the question. If you want to paint your living room lime-green and your bedroom slate-gray, so be it! If you want to pair a mid-century modern couch with a Victorian-era coffee table, then that's what you're gonna do! Sometimes these unusual pairings end up being inspired, other times they'll seem like you're gunning for a spot on the show *Hoarders*. Speaking of hoarding, Pisces' sentimentality means you love to keep everything, from ticket stubs, to tickets for movies you didn't even like, to cords for devices that have been obsolete for decades. Every inch of the Pisces abode is cluttered with knickknacks, baubles, and papers you could have tossed out years ago. But you never know! Those Beanie Babies still might make a comeback.

PISCES AND TRAVEL

When a Pisces travels they let whimsy and romance be their guide. While this may sound like the start of a great novel, their laziness and decision-fatigue kicks in the moment they have to deal with the aspects of travel that conveniently get left out of your favorite "Eat, Pray, Love" adventures. Specifically, booking flights, securing hotel rooms, and doing anything other than dreaming about being swept off your feet by an attractive stranger in a foreign land. Pisces loves to dream about romantic vacations to far-flung locations, but lacks the basic motivation to make these trips a reality. When you do take a trip (usually because it was planned by someone else), you're always at risk of coming down with an acute case of Paris Syndrome (i.e. an extreme malaise brought on by the fact that your destination will never quite match up to the idealized version you built up in your head). The fantasy just never seems to account for things like currency exchanges, flight delays, or figuring out how to navigate the metro.

The two sides of Pisces

Pisces is represented by two fish being pulled in opposite directions, which is a perfect way to describe the influence of their dark masculine and dark feminine sides. Though Pisces is classified as one of the Zodiac's feminine signs, it's dark masculine is always there, pulling Pisces in its own direction. Here's what to expect when one of these two combating fish gets its way.

PISCES DARK MASCULINE

A Pisces that has let its dark masculine fish take the lead is one who will never hold back when it comes to expressing their feelings. They see their self-expression as a God-given right and are prone to emotional outbursts. They prioritize feelings over facts, making them extremely hard to deal with when their emotional response is being challenged. To a Pisces that's swimming in the dark masculine pool, if they feel something is true, it is true, regardless of what anyone else has to say to the contrary.

PISCES DARK FEMININE

When Pisces' dark feminine fish takes the lead, they can often become lost in a sea of reverie. This version of Pisces would rather sit around all day dreaming about their ideal life than take any action to make it happen. In their ideal world, all their dreaming and pining will one day be rewarded by a handsome savior who appears out of thin air to solve all of their problems. It's a nice idea, but it's actually quite hard to meet your Prince Charming when you are locked up in a tower daydreaming all day—no matter what Rapunzel may tell you.

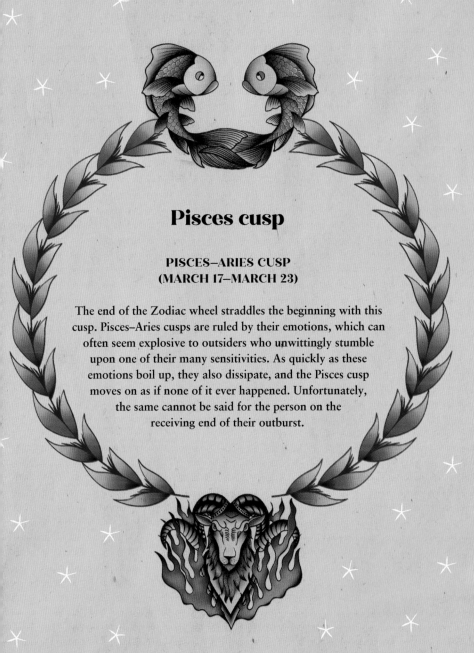

Pisces cusp

PISCES–ARIES CUSP
(MARCH 17–MARCH 23)

The end of the Zodiac wheel straddles the beginning with this cusp. Pisces–Aries cusps are ruled by their emotions, which can often seem explosive to outsiders who unwittingly stumble upon one of their many sensitivities. As quickly as these emotions boil up, they also dissipate, and the Pisces cusp moves on as if none of it ever happened. Unfortunately, the same cannot be said for the person on the receiving end of their outburst.

Index

A

air signs 11
Aquarius 134–45
  cusp 145
  dark feminine 144
  dark masculine 144
  in the family 142
  at home 143
  modality 12
  in a nutshell 136–7
  placements 138
  in a relationship 140
  single 139
  and travel 143
  at work 142
Aries 14–25
  cusp 25
  dark feminine 24
  dark masculine 24
  in the family 22
  at home 23
  modality 12
  in a nutshell 16–17
  placements 18
  in a relationship 20
  single 19
  and travel 23
  at work 22

B

"big three" signs 13

C

Cancer 50–61
  cusp 61
  dark feminine 60
  dark masculine 60
  in the family 58
  at home 59
  modality 12
  in a nutshell 52–3
  placements 54
  in a relationship 56
  single 55
  and travel 59
  at work 58
Capricorn 122–33
  cusp 133
  dark feminine 132
  dark masculine 132
  in the family 130
  at home 131
  modality 12
  in a nutshell 124–5
  placements 126
  in a relationship 128
  single 127
  and travel 131
  at work 130
cardinal modality 10

E

Earth signs 11
elements 11

F

fire signs 11
fixed modality 12

G

Gemini 38–49
  cusp 49
  dark feminine 48
  dark masculine 48
  in the family 47
  at home 46
  modality 12
  in a nutshell 40–1
  placements 42
  in a relationship 44
  single 43
  and travel 47
  at work 46

J

Jupiter 9

K

key concepts 9–13

L

Leo 62–73
  cusp 73
  dark feminine 72
  dark masculine 72
  in the family 70
  at home 71
  modality 12
  in a nutshell 64–5
  placements 66
  in a relationship 68
  single 67
  and travel 71
  at work 70
Libra 86–97
  cusp 97
  dark feminine 96
  dark masculine 96

in the family 94
at home 95
modality 10
in a nutshell 88–9
placements 90
in a relationship 92
single 91
and travel 95
at work 94

M
Mars 9
Mercury 9
modality 12
Moon, the 10
Moon signs 13
mutable modality 12

N
Neptune 10

O
opposing signs 13

P
Pisces 146–57
  cusp 157
  dark feminine 156
  dark masculine 156
  in the family 154
  at home 155
  modality 12
  in a nutshell 148–9
  placements 150
  in a relationship 152
  single 151

and travel 155
at work 154
Pluto 10

R
rising signs 13
ruling planets 9–10

S
Sagittarius 110–21
  cusp 121
  dark feminine 120
  dark masculine 120
  in the family 118
  at home 119
  modality 12
  in a nutshell 112–13
  placements 114
  in a relationship 116
  single 115
  and travel 119
  at work 118
Saturn 7
Scorpio 98–109
  cusp 109
  dark feminine 108
  dark masculine 108
  in the family 106
  at home 107
  modality 12
  in a nutshell 100–1
  placements 102
  in a relationship 104
  single 103
  and travel 107
  at work 106
Sun, the 10

T
Taurus 26–37
  cusp 37
  dark feminine 36
  dark masculine 36
  in the family 34
  at home 35
  modality 12
  in a nutshell 28–9
  placements 30
  in a relationship 32
  single 31
  and travel 35
  at work 34

U
Uranus 10

V
Venus 9, 13
Virgo 74–85
  cusp 85
  dark feminine 84
  dark masculine 84
  in the family 82
  at home 83
  modality 12
  in a nutshell 76–7
  placements 78
  in a relationship 80
  single 79
  and travel 83
  at work 82

W
water signs 11

Credits

Nazarii M/Shutterstock.com; Anastasiia Veretennikova; Shutterstock.com; Christos Georghiou/Shutterstock.com

About the illustrator

Bruna Carla da Silva is a Brazilian artist and illustrator, based in Liverpool, United Kingdom. Through digital art and paintings on canvas and fabrics, she expresses her passion for the feminine world in a traditional tattoo style. You can find out more about Bruna at sailorbroo.com and on social media @sailor_broo.

Author acknowledgments

I could never have written this book without the wonderful team at Quarto, particularly my editor Charlene Fernandes, who guided me through the process from across the pond. I am forever grateful to my sister Natalie for introducing me to all things woo and for never shying away from a conversation about planetary movements, birth charts, or vibes. I'd also love to thank my wonderful parents, Felix and Deborah, who have never batted an eye at any of my endeavors, astrological or comedic.

This book is also dedicated to my dear friends, Kady Ruth, Bailey, and Tyler, who never got annoyed when I'd send them snippets of the roast of their sign (at least to my face) and my wonderful husband Danny, who, despite being a Scorpio, fills my life with joy, laughter, and lightness every day. And to my wonderful pets, Rusty (dog, Sagittarius) and Biz (cat, Libra) who have never shown any interest in astrology or comedy but are always up for a cuddle after a long day of writing.